ASCENSION TO INFINITY

THE HIDDEN TREASURES OF PRAYER

AYATOLLAH MISBAH YAZDI
TRANSLATED BY ZAID ALSALAMI

Originally published in 2004 in Farsi
This English edition is published in 2024

Author: Ayatollah Muhammad Taqi Misbah Yazdi
Translator: Sheikh Dr. Zaid Alsalami
Editor: Hamid Tehrani

ISBN: 9781738494934

Ahlulbayt
Islamic
Mission

بِسْمِ ٱللَّهِ ٱلرَّحْمَٰنِ ٱلرَّحِيمِ

In the name of God, the Merciful,
the Compassionate

Contents

Translator's Note 7

Introduction 13

Some Points on the Topic of Prayer 14

About this Book 16

Chapter One: Inner-attention to God in Prayer 19

The Importance of Acquiring Inner-attention to God in Prayer 19

Methods of Acquiring Inner-attention to God in Prayer 21

Chapter Two: Sincerity in Prayer 33

The Status of Sincerity in Prayer 33

'Allāmah al-Majlisī on Gaining Closeness to God in Prayer 34

Showing Off Nullifies Prayer 36

Showing Off 40

Signs of Sincerity and Showing Off (Feigning Virtuousness) 43

Hidden Showing Off 46

A Story about Showing Off and Sincerity 49

Chapter Three: The Spirit of Prayer 51

The Real Prayer 51

Three Steps Towards Obtaining the Spirit and Reality of Prayer 55

Methods to Achieve Presence of the Heart in Prayer 64

Obtaining the State of Humility in Prayer 71

The Relation Between Love and Humility 85

Ways of Producing *Khushū'* in Prayer 94

Chapter Four: On the Doorstep of the Beloved 119

The Role of Intention in Human Elevation or Fall 119

Intention and its Levels 123

Types of Intentions 125

A Correct and Accepted Intention........ 127
A Practical Step Towards Correcting Intentions........ 131
Levels of a Lofty Intention........ 136
The Gradual Process in Completing the Intention........ 139
A look into Adhān........ 141
Some Important Questions........ 153
Chapter Five: An Accepted Prayer........ 169
Conditions of an Accepted Prayer........ 170
Effects of an Accepted Prayer........ 174
A Final Question........ 176

Translator's Note

THE MODERN WORLD advances forth with fast-paced changes, but perhaps too fast for comfort. Technological progress has made many aspects of our lives easier, connecting our world together and relieving us of many difficulties. Yet, our society has evolved into something that we either love or hate. Compared with the past, we have never experienced what we now have. Cultures and ideas easily cross borders, as what used to be confined within a nation has now become global and accessible for everyone to adopt. One could be in a completely isolated part of the world, but still be strongly influenced by someone, or something, in a completely different part. We all benefit from our new 'global village', but this most certainly does not mean we are now better-off than we were before.

We all face greater problems in the environmental, mental, and moral domains. Looking at the current state of mental health in today's society explains much about our predicament as we need just only to refer to statistics to realise what kind of crisis we are in.[1] As for moral decadence, it could not be any worse. With the decay of ethical values and overall human decency, something that was always seen as a universal, moral principle is now questioned, challenged, and even socially rejected. Moral corruption and debauchery are flagrantly common and ever so prevailing in the public eye.

In all this chaos, many are trying to find ways of alleviating this mental health predicament and moral degradation by either separating themselves from urban life entirely or looking into what religions have to offer. Religion, too, though, has not been free from criticism. Many not only outright condemn it, but most also blame it for society's problems.

With our instinctive need to satisfy our mental and spiritual aspects, aspects which are utterly bankrupt in Western society, many have gone in search of means to address those issues that pertain to the soul. Those who resort to recreational drugs and alcohol consumption do so because of their ubiquitous accessibility and almost immediate results in numbing their feelings and escaping from reality.

A simple internet search shows humanity's appalling situation. It is estimated that one in four people, globally, will experience a mental health condition in their lifetime. The United Nations records that almost one million people commit suicide per year, as the predominant mental health problem is due to anxiety and depression.

In the West, Eastern religions and traditions have been popular as of late, for numerous reasons, but mostly because of what Western society lacks in addressing the needs of the soul. Buddhism, for instance, has been pervasive amongst Westerners, with a special interest in certain personalities like the Dalai Lama. People are in search of 'gurus' to be inspired by them, or would even join the International Society for Krishna Consciousness (ISKCON), for example. Yoga, in particular, has been very popular; and although its origin was finding calmness in life, it is now overwhelmingly exclusive for elitists and has now degenerated into a fitness-focused activity. Interestingly, a large portion of those who have adopted these trends still continue their hedonistic lifestyle, where they take only what suits them and discard whatever affects their secular and individualistic life.

All of this is due to an ongoing neglect of our mental and spiritual well-being in Western society, resulting in this pandemic of moral and spiritual decadence. People are desperately looking for solutions to heal their psychological instabilities and trauma. We all must come together and not only address the mental and spiritual health issue, but offer real solutions—solutions that are tried, tested, and true. In Islam, the final and most-complete religion, everything that is embedded within the fabric of human nature is holistically related to one another: the physical is related to the spiritual; the body is connected to the soul. Whatever we think and believe is tantamount to influence our ternary existence of spirit, soul, and body. This is why, generally speaking, religion and being *actively* religious contributes to much better mental health, allowing one to overcome life's stressful situations. However, not all religions have what it needs to satisfy our mental and spiritual conditions or even offer effective, long-term solutions. Islam, through the plenary way of the *Ahl al-Bayt*, penetrates into the very essence of the human condition, giving all the necessary provisions needed in order to navigate the many turbulences of life.

The teachings of the *Ahl al-Bayt* purvey to each-and-every existential need: physical, moral, mental, and spiritual. It is the *Shīʿī* path which gives that strongly structured worldview, firmly aligned with the original *fiṭrī* disposition, and whatever else is needed in order to achieve that serenity and inner-calm. It is the *Shīʿī* path that truly teaches that God is Perfectly Just (*al-ʿĀdil*) and that we have an equilibrium of "predestination" and "freewill". Knowing this produces a resolute mindset, allowing one to deal with those indefinite challenges faced in life. Should one experience any hardship or calamity, it is that salvific knowledge inculcated from the impeccable *Imāms* that gives one meaning to what one is enduring. We interpret what we suffer in an affirmative way, not allowing it to break our spirit or affect our mental health.

This way of dealing with mental instabilities and challenges dates back far earlier than the young, modern science of psychology which only emerged as an independent discipline in the 19th century. Why do so many ridicule the religious when the latter suggest that resorting to religious remedies for mental health is more efficacious than medicine or therapy administered by modern psychologists? What were people doing before modern psychology? The point here is that spiritual health and spiritual medicine has always been there and is a fundamental focus of Islam. One's mindset and spiritual outlook, especially one's view on life, has a direct effect on one's mental health, having a strong reflection on feelings, emotions, and other personal or social reactions.

When we have meaning and value for life, we aspire to reach its goals for perfection and complete the purpose for which we were created. We take care of ourselves and we take care of others; we take care of others as if they are our own self and we take care of our own self as if we are responsible for another. Whatever ordeal or crisis we face, or any physical or mental illness, or when we get old to the point of death, we turn to our firmly structured worldview. A correct worldview—with a firmly grounded and healthy intellect—will therefore directly influence one's behaviour and outlook on life. Muslims then are indeed blessed to have this.

Islam focuses on spiritual growth, pursued through the most-effective way, which is nothing other than the daily prayers. As we have yet to delve deeper into the mysteries of prayer, we should at least begin to gain a better understanding of what we regularly practice every single day. It is for this reason that the book in your hands, *Ascension to Infinity* is imperative to read. It explains the spiritual dimensions and benefits of prayer by giving a unique insight into the preliminaries, the intention, the wordings, and the very actions performed in prayer.

The late author, Professor Muḥammad-Taqī Miṣbāḥ Yazdī (1935–2021),[1] explained these topics in such a profound and practical way. Of course, as an authority in both the rational sciences (*al-ʿulūm al-ʿaqliyyah*) and the transmitted sciences (*al-ʿulūm al-naqliyyah*), he simplified complex, technical, and deep concepts on prayer, making it easy for readers of all levels to understand and cherish. It is certain that anyone who reads this book will greatly profit from it and improve their quality of prayer.

1. Muḥammad-Taqī Miṣbāḥ al-Yazdī was born on Thursday, 25 Shawwāl, 1353 H / 31 January, 1935 in Yazd, Pahlavī Iran and joined the theological seminary at the young age of fifteen—first in al-Najaf in Iraq for seven-months and then later relocated to Qum, Iran for the remainder of his life. He had studied and completed all of the related sciences under great scholars and luminaries such as: al-Sayyid Ḥusayn al-Ṭabaʾṭabaʾī al-Burūjirdī ? (1292–1380 H / 1875–1961), Imām al-Sayyid Rūḥ-Allah al-Mūsawī al-Khumaynī (1320–1409 H / 1902–1989), al-ʿAllāmah al-Sayyid Muḥammad-Ḥusayn al-Ṭabaʾṭabaʾī (1320–1402 H / 1903–1981), and most notably under al-Shaykh "al-ʿAbd" Muḥammad-Taqī al-Bahjat al-Fūmanī (1334–1430 H / 1916–2009)—all of whom were great gnostics and notable mystics (*ʿurafāʾ*). Professor Miṣbāḥ Yazdī authored numerous books, taught various subjects, held many official positions within the government of the Islāmic Republic of Iran, and in 1991 founded the prestigious Imam Khomeini Education and Research Institute (Muʾassasihyi Āmūzishī va Pizhūhishīyi Imām Khumaynī) based in Qum. He passed-away, making his final ascension to the Infinite, on the evening of Friday, 17 Jumādā al-Awwal, 1442 H / 1 January, 2021 at the age of eighty-five. He is buried beside his belovèd teacher, al-Shaykh al-Bahjat, within the sacred mausoleum (*ḥaram*) of al-Sayyidah Fāṭimah al-Maʿṣūmah (ʿa) in Qum.

This book is a series of selected excerpts taken from the various lectures delivered by the late author on the topic of the spiritual ascent in prayer. It was originally compiled in Persian by Sayyid Muḥammad-Riḍā Ghiyāthī Kirmānī with the title *'Urūj tā Bī-nahāyat* (عـروج تـا بی‌نهایـت).[2] We are grateful to the Ahlulbayt Islamic Mission (AIM) and Sayyid Samir al-Haidari , for the choice in rendering this book into English and taking the responsibility of all the necessary requirements for publishing it. We are also grateful to everyone who assisted in the initial drafts of the translation and to all those who contributed in editing, proofreading, reviewing, and giving their invaluable suggestions for improving the text for publication.

May God enlighten our hearts through our prayers
and illuminate the Straight Path to Him,
living prosperously for His sake,
and enjoying His endless
bounties under His infinite Mercy.

Āmīn

Zaid Alsalami

زَيْد السَّلَامِي

2. Published by the Imam Khomeini Research and Education Institute (Qum, 1383 SH / 2004). For this translation, we used the fifth edition published in 1388 SH / 2009. We also consulted the Arabic translation rendered by Sayyid 'Abbās Nūr al-Dīn entitled *al-'Urūj ilā al-Lā-nihāyah* (Dār al-Ma'ārif al-Ḥikmiyyah: Beirut, 1439 H/2017).

Introduction

By Sayyid Muḥammad Riḍā Ghiyāthī Kermānī

A believer is described as being as firm as a mountain and someone who cannot be shaken by storms of events and calamities. What grants a believer such astounding firmness and sturdiness is connecting to the Origin of existence, the Core of Infinite Omnipotence and Source of Eternal Glory.

Those who, within the pounding ocean of the events around them, have tied the vessel of their heart to the firm rope of God cannot be tossed about by its high waves or destabilised by its riptides.

Indeed, this describes those who feel comfort when remembering God, acquiring inner-peace, calmness and tranquillity.

It is beyond question that prayer is the greatest form of remembrance of God, as the Almighty has said in the Quran:

﴿وَأَقِمِ الصَّلاةَ لِذِكرِي﴾

And maintain the prayer for My remembrance.[3]

---

3. Quran, 20:14.

In removing the veils of this secret of prayer, we are invited to this dominion of tranquillity, amid a life occupied with clamour and noise, specifically in a challenging era of competing in the field of technology and advancement. These believers can hear a melodious tune playing in the ears of their souls, saying:

﴿أَلَا بِذِكْرِ اللَّهِ تَطْمَئِنُّ الْقُلُوبُ﴾

Indeed! The hearts find rest in God's remembrance![4]

Some Points on the Topic of Prayer

Regarding the topic of prayer, a few points should be mentioned:

(1) The reality of prayer is defined as a connection between God and His servant, and without purity, one is not fit to be in His presence. Hence, it is necessary for us to perform ablution and prepare for prayer with a pure body.

(2) Spiritual sages have said that ablution must be performed with deliberation and veneration as one must pay attention to its secrets. This is because the presence of one's heart in prayer is equal to the presence of one's heart when they are performing the ablution.

(3) Prior to commencing prayer, one must vacate their heart from every worldly matter that would bring about any form of mental distraction. This is so that the person praying understands what they are saying and not to be under the intoxication of inattentiveness so as to avoid being included among the addressees of the verse:

4. Quran, 13:28.

﴿لا تَقرَبُوا الصَّلاةَ وَأَنتُم سُكارىٰ﴾

Do not approach prayer when you are intoxicated.[5]

It is for this reason it has been said:

If it's time for dinner (*al-ʿashāʾ*) and night prayer (*al-ʿishāʾ*), put dinner first.[6]

(4) Recommended acts should be performed before starting prayer to remove the blemishes of the heart. The inner aspect of the person praying will acquire the quality of an intimate supplication and be overwhelmed with Holy Divine Gusts (*nafaḥāt al-quds al-ilāhī*) and the descending of infinite blessings.

(5) It is encouraged to participate in congregational prayer as when believers congregate together their souls are unified. If one of the participants praying is inattentive, and the rest are attentive in their prayer, the congregation will compensate for the inattentive one and complete the deficiencies of their prayer.

(6) Due to the extreme level of mercy the Messenger of God (ṣ) had over his umma, he wanted his people to acquire the state and condition that he personally experienced on the night of his Heavenly Ascension (*miʿrāj*). When the Prophet (ṣ) reached Divine proximity, he requested that this honour would also

---

5. Quran, 4:43.
6. The narration is:
إذا حَضَرَ العَشَاء والعِشاء فابْدَؤُوا بالعَشاءِ
This is a narration attributed to the Prophet (ṣ). It basically means eat your
dinner so that you are not distracted by hunger while you are praying
See: Abū al-Qāsim al-Qummī, *Ghanāʾim al-ayām fi masāʾil al-ḥalāl wa al-ḥarām*, (Khurāsān: Maktab al-Iʿlām al-Islāmī, 1417 AH) v. 5, p. 351.

be gifted to his umma. This prayer, which was the form of his own state, accompanied him back from his ascending journey in order to be shared with his umma, and that is why prayer is said to be "the ascension (*miʿrāj*) of the believer".

(7) Prayer is one of God's greatest sanctities and entering this sanctified state commences with the sacred glorifying (*takbīratul-iḥrām*) and finishes with salutations (*al-salām*). Each section and part of the prayer is one of the divine unveilings and a distinctive invitation from the All-Merciful.

It is unfortunate for someone to enter this sanctified state and leave inattentively, without having witnessed, spoken or benefitted from such a blessing.

(8) Prayer in its outer form holds the secret to the worshipping of all angels. Some angels are in constant bowing, some are in constant prostration, some are in the state of standing, some are in the state of sitting, some are in the state of seeking forgiveness, some are in the state of reciting. Some angels are glorifying, some are praising, some are sending salutations to the Prophet (ṣ). It is for this reason that in each of these acts the person praying is in synchronisation with the angels.

About this Book

It is beyond any doubt that the most beautiful and loftiest of statements about prayer are those given by the holy Prophet (ṣ) and his noble progeny (ʿa). In turn, the heirs of these immaculate beings sought to benefit from such beauty, quenching their thirst for the truth by drinking from their pond of knowledge.

One of these heirs is Ayatullah Miṣbāḥ Yazdī, an eminent scholar who was solid in his devotion to knowledge, culture, intuition and faith. He was an example for the Prophetic hadith:

مَـنْ أَخْلَـصَ اَلْعِبَـادَةَ لِلَّهِ أَرْبَـعِينَ صَبَاحـاً ظَهَـرَتْ يَنَابِيـعُ اَلْحِكْمَـةِ مِـنْ قَلْبِـهِ عَلَى لِسَـانِهِ

Whosoever shows sincerity to God for forty mornings, fountains of wisdom will flow from his heart over to his tongue.[7]

Fountains of wisdom flowed from his heart and tongue to those eagerly yearning for it. Ayatullah Miṣbāḥ Yazdī left behind many eternal books, and these books became an example for:

﴿عَينًا يَشرَبُ بِها عِبادُ اللَّهِ﴾

A spring where the servants of God drink from.[8]

This book is one of these works, compiled from his writings and lectures on the topic of prayer, hoping that the Almighty will accept it from us, to assist us, especially on:

﴿يَومَ لا يَنفَعُ مالٌ وَلا بَنونَ﴾

The day when neither wealth nor children will be of no avail.[9]

We anticipate the hastening in the relieving reappearance of the Awaited Saviour of this world, Imām al-Mahdī, may our souls be sacrificed for him. We also wish the well-being and prolonged life of the leader of the Islamic Republic of Iran, Ayatullah Khamenei.

---

7. *Al-Wāfī*, vol. 1, p. 10. *Biḥār al-Anwār*, vol. 53, p. 326.
8. Quran, 76:6.
9. Quran, 26:88.

Chapter One
Inner-attention to God in Prayer

The Importance of Acquiring Inner-attention to God in Prayer

Before commencing the prayer, it is best to turn thoughts and ideas away from material things or anything that would distract one's senses and have complete concentration on God in prayer. If one is to pray alone, they must try to find somewhere that is quiet and does not have any paintings or pictures that would attract their attention. If they want to pray in congregation, they must position themselves among the people praying in such a way that does not divert them or break their connection with God. It should be as if they are lost within the crowd.

The invocations that are recited within the prayer carry numerous concepts that must be reflected in the mind, but attention is not among the category of statements or concepts. Attention, rather, is from the category of presential and intuitive knowledge, endowed by God's Grace to those who have perceived the presence of their Lord.

In light of the power and potential that Almighty God endows upon the human being, one can turn to their Lord from the depths of their heart while reciting these invocations in the prayer and conceive its meanings. In most situations we do not bear the necessary aptitude to have inner-attention to God, but if we were to implore and beseech Him and also concentrate on the concepts in what we say in prayer, we will be able to create such a spiritual state in ourselves or even strengthen it. This inner-attention of the heart occurs in a limited form and in special states for most people, and it therefore becomes important to increase this attention and also intensify and deepen it.

For most people, at times while supplicating and imploring God, that state occurs in a limited form where they go beyond the concepts and statements to become completely attentive of who they are addressing, as if they see Him. They completely forget what surrounds them, as if they have forgotten themselves. If such a state of attentiveness to God were to happen to us, we must strive to strengthen it and keep it consistent. This kind of inner-attention of the heart to God is something invaluable, so we must pay what is necessary to keep this precious state. We must first put in effort and aim at creating this state within ourselves, and then work towards cementing and preserving it.

Methods of Acquiring Inner-attention to God in Prayer

1. Attention to the Absolute Grandness of God

One way of bringing about the heart's attention to God and acquiring a state of veneration (*khuḍūʿ*) and humility (*khushūʿ*) is paying attention to the absolute grandness (*ʿaẓamah*) of God and to perceive the lowliness of one's self. Through witnessing God's bounties and through conceptualising the greatness of His creation, we comprehend some aspects of the greatness of God. Whatever way we expand our minds and summon the image of how great this material world is, our perception of the greatness of God is insignificant and nowhere close to the grandness of this world. The mightiness of the created realm is such that the distance between two stars is equal to millions of light years, and we cannot even perceive the distance of one lightyear, so how are we able to perceive millions of light years.

We can try to conceptualise God's grandness by visualising a great massive space, or a large vast desert or a great deep ocean, and then compare our small insignificant bodies to it. We can ask this question while comparing; what does our body make up in relation to this large material world that we are able to conceive. The result we end up with in this comparison could be that if we were to compare our bodies with this material world it would be an insignificant existence that cannot be seen by other than a microscope. What would then be the case for other worlds that we have no ability to perceive how great they are!

Making such a physical and material comparison predominantly shows our spiritual inferiority and how weak and trivial we are. However, although this human is an inferior insignificant being, Almighty God granted it a spiritual element that can establish itself within the radiance of recognising God and achieving connection with Him.

There are also supplications recommended to recite before prayer that hold valuable points that can help us fulfil our prayer in the best and most complete form if we observe them. Among these points, considered the most important of them, is paying attention to the realm of divinity and the grandeur of God, along with seeing the human being as insignificant and inferior. Such an approach is important and effective, which is why it has been stressed that a person about to pray should commence their prayer with seven *takbīrs*, pronouncing six *takbīrs* before *takbīratul-iḥrām*.

There are narrations that explain the reason behind the recommendation of seven *takbīrs* before commencing prayer. The holy Prophet (ṣ) was about to pray, and Imam Husayn (ʿa) was beside him. The Prophet (ṣ) performed the *takbīr*, but Imam Husain (ʿa) was not able to do it in the correct form. So the Prophet (ṣ) repeated the *takbīr* again and again correcting Imam Husayn (ʿa). After the Prophet (ṣ) reached the seventh *takbīr*, Imam Husayn (ʿa) was able to perform the seventh takbīr in the correct form, and from then onwards the seven *takbīrs* became recommended at the beginning of prayer.[10]

---

10. Al-Majlisī, *Biḥār al-Anwār,* vol. 44, p. 194.
Furthermore, the recommendation and emphasis on the seven takbīrs at the beginning of prayer which is considered as turning attention to the greatness of the realm of divinity and insignificance of the human in front of it came about as a result of the takbīr perform by the Prophet (ṣ) to teach Imām Ḥusain (ʿa). In turn, we also perform other acts of worship that have come as a result of actions from God's vicegerents and have become either recommended or obligatory. An example for this is in the hajj pilgrimage rite and the obligatory rite of *saʿyī* between Ṣafā and Marwa. It has been mentioned that the philosophy behind this rite becoming obligatory was when Hajar, the wife of Prophet Ibrahim, was striving to find water to quench her son Ismail who was thirsty, she frequented between the two hills of Ṣafā

2. Turning Attention to God's Absolute Grace to Humankind

If someone were to help us at our time of need or offer us some money when we are in financial strain, we would consider ourselves forever grateful and thankful to them, and also try not to spend this money on something that would upset them. Although Almighty God has granted us innumerable blessings, we not only do not consider or value them but rather feel that He owes us and we do not hesitate in dismissing His bounties (*kufr al-ni'ma*) or disobeying Him. We might even use these divine blessings in a way that would lead to His wrath and discontent. If we were not loyal to our friends and were the source of hurting them, they would distance themselves from us, unfriend us and not show us their nice side after that.

At the same time, with all our disobedience, aversion and disloyalty to our Lord, showing lack of respect to the realm of the Lord of the worlds and our ungratefulness to His bounties, He still does not expel

---

and Marwa. When she would arrive at Ṣafā, she would see the mirage of water at Marwa, and when she went towards Marwa, she would see the mirage of water at Ṣafā. She rushed to and fro seven times between the two hills, and on the seventh time while returning to Ṣafā she saw water springing out from under Prophet Ismail's feet. It is for this reason, in following by example what Hajar did, that it has become obligatory for us as Muslims when in Hajj to perform *sa'yī* between Ṣafā and Marwa. The same is with staying in Minā and offering a sacrifice there, also in respect to Prophet Ibrahim ('a) and following him when Almighty God ordered him to slaughter his son Ismail and offer him as a sacrifice. When Ibrahim ('a) passed his divine exam, God brought down a great ram for him to sacrifice. We now perform this as an obligatory part of our Hajj pilgrimage. What we have mentioned with the Prophet (ṣ) teaching Imām Ḥusain ('a) in how to correctly perform the takbīr is not something far-fetched from being authentic. Legislating the recommendation of saying the takbīrs seven times at the commencing of prayer could be due to this particular incident, and it also shows us how great the status of Imām Ḥusain ('a) was, and for us to remember him in our prayer as well.

us far away from His presence, but rather He still accepts us. If we were to go to our friend and ask them to forgive us, when meeting them and wanting to speak to them, we cannot be careless or inattentive towards them. However, with all our disobedience to God and with the sins we commit, we turn to implore Him and remember Him with our tongues while our hearts are directed somewhere else.

It is like when we have a need and turn to the divine Lordship, we give our backs to Him and turn away from Him. Such behaviour is indeed the highest level of insolence and lowliness from a servant towards God. Almighty God is the manifestation of perfection, beauty, grace, absolute forgiveness and He continues to accept us with all our vile behaviour. In fact, our repentance and returning to the Almighty actually brings indescribable happiness to Him.

It is narrated from Abū ʿUbaydah al-Ḥadhdhā'[11] that he heard Imām Muḥammad al-Bāqir (ʿa) say:

إِنَّ اَللَّهَ تَعَالَى أَشَدُّ فَرَحاً بِتَوْبَةِ عَبْدِهِ مِنْ رَجُلٍ أَضَلَّ رَاحِلَتَهُ وَ زَادَهُ فِي لَيْلَةٍ ظَلْمَاءَ فَوَجَدَهَا فَاللَّهُ أَشَدُّ فَرَحاً بِتَوْبَةِ عَبْدِهِ مِنْ ذَلِكَ اَلرَّجُلِ بِرَاحِلَتِهِ حِينَ وَجَدَهَا

Verily Almighty God becomes extremely happy with the repentance of His servant, more than a man who had lost his riding camel and his provisions on a dark night and then finds it. God is happier when His servant repents, more than someone who loses his riding camel then finds it.[12]

11. His name was Ziyād ibn ʿĪsā, from Kufah and a reliable trustworthy companion of Imām al-Bāqir (a.s.).
12. Al-Kulaynī, *al-Kāfī*, ed. ʿAlīi Akbar Ghaffārī (Tehran: Dār al-Kutub al-Islāmiyyah, ed. 3, 1368 SY), vol. 2, ch. repentance, p. 438, ḥ. 8.

If for a period of time we were to train ourselves in prayer to mentally summon God's greatness, bounties and grace, and how abased this world is, such attention to these concepts will gradually become a habitual state. We will be able to effortlessly bring this state about and, ultimately, will achieve a greater and loftier benefit from our prayer. When someone feels comfortable with certain practices and beliefs, they become consistent in upholding them. Almighty God grants them the ability for one to simultaneously conceptualise all these momentums, thoughts and practices so that they are comfortable with, and attentive to, them.

These lofty monotheistic concepts are manifested in the following supplication that has been recommended to be recited after the fifth *takbīr* before prayer:

لَبَّيْكَ وَسَعْدَيْكَ وَٱلْخَيْرُ فِي يَدَيْكَ وَٱلشَّرُّ لَيْسَ إِلَيْكَ
وَٱلْمَهْدِيُّ مَنْ هَدَيْتَ عَبْدُكَ وَٱبْنُ عَبْدَيْكَ بَيْنَ يَدَيْكَ
مِنْكَ وَبِكَ وَلَكَ وَإِلَيْكَ لاَ مَلْجَأَ وَلاَ مَنْجَى وَلاَ مَفَرَّ
مِنْكَ إِلاَّ إِلَيْكَ سُبْحَانَكَ وَحَنَانَيْكَ تَبَارَكْتَ وَتَعَالَيْتَ
سُبْحَانَكَ رَبَّ ٱلْبَيْتِ ٱلْحَرَامِ

I am here at Your service. All good is in Your hands and you are far away from evil. The guided is he whom You have guided. Your servant, the son of Your servant is in front of You, from You, to You and for You. There is no sanctuary from You except with You, and no fleeing from You other than to You. All glory be Yours. You are the Blessed and Sublime. All glory to You, Lord of the Sacred House.[13]

13. *Biḥār al-Anwār*, vol. 81, p. 366. *Mafātīḥ al-Jinān, duā' al-takbīrāt.*

3. Understanding the Greatness of How God Receives His Servant

There is a significant point that is rarely considered but we must keep it in mind. When someone goes to visit a highly respected figure and that figure welcomes them and is ready to listen to and fulfil their needs, they would feel very fortunate. This is because the renowned figure who may be occupied with important and pressing matters, was willing to take the time out and meet with the visitor. What blessed success is greater than Almighty God receiving a person, intimately conversing with them, and including them in His blessing and grace? We must therefore be very grateful for this grace and divine care, which is what we can see in the statements and supplications of our immaculate Imāms when they confide to God and thank Him for these great blessings.

One of these supplications has been recommended to recite prior to commencing prayer, and it is:

اَللَّهُمَّ أَقْبِلْ إِلَيَّ بِوَجْهِكَ وَأُقْبِلُ إِلَيْكَ بِقَلْبِي اَللَّهُمَّ أَعِنِّي عَلَى ذِكْرِكَ وَشُكْرِكَ وَحُسْنِ عِبَادَتِكَ اَلْحَمْدُ لِلَّهِ اَلَّذِي جَعَلَنِي مِمَّنْ يُنَاجِيهِ

> O God, turn to me with Your face, and I will turn to You with my heart. O God, help me remember You, to be grateful to You, and to worship You in an excellent manner. Praise be to God who has made me among those who supplicate to Him.[14]

In al-Munājāt al-Shaʿbāniyah the worshipper is also asking God to turn to him while praying and supplicating to Him, and for the Almighty to receive him and not distance him away from His realm:

---

14. *Biḥār al-Anwār,* vol. 81, p. 365. *Falāḥ al-Sāʾil,* vol. 1, p. 91.

أَللّٰهُمَّ صَلِّ عَلَىٰ مُحَمَّدٍ وَآلِ مُحَمَّدٍ، وَسْمَعْ دُعَائِي إِذَا دَعَوْتُكَ،
وَسْمَعْ نِدَائِي إِذَا نَادَيْتُكَ، وَأَقْبِلْ عَلَيَّ إِذَا نَاجَيْتُكَ، فَقَدْ هَرَبْتُ
إِلَيْكَ، وَوَقَفْتُ بَيْنَ يَدَيكَ مُسْتَكِيناً لَكَ مُتَضَرِّعاً إِلَيْكَ

O God, send salutations upon Muhammad and his Progeny. Listen to my supplication when I pray to You, listen to my call when I call upon You, accept me when I confide to You. I have escaped towards You, stand submissively before You and imploring You.[15]

In the supplications to be recited prior to commencing prayer, with God allowing His servant to converse with Him, the worshipper is requesting from God to attend to him. Naturally, God attends to all His creation, but of course this occurs on different grades, and not all are on the same level.

An example of this is when a group visits a distinguished spiritual leader or a *Marjaʿ Taqlīd*, they would be looking at the group, we would also receive a glance specifically at us as well. The esteemed figure would not be looking exclusively at us, but then out of everyone, they may glance directly at us. Such a glance is certainly different to any other glance, and it comes from their special care and grace to each individual. It indicates their contentment and not having any criticism or complaint against us.

Almighty God attends to all of His creation and encompasses all existence, with nothing hidden from His knowledge as He sees everything. But there is a big difference between God's attention to oppressors, like Shimr and Yazīd, and His attention to His prophets and saints. There is also a big difference between God's attention to us, and His attention to Salmān al-Fārisī, Abū Dharr and other righteous

---

15. *Mafātīḥ al-Jinān, al-Munājāt al-Shaʿbāniyah.*

people upon whom God has sent His salutations through Gabriel, with the Prophet delegated to convey His greetings to them.

If we were to reach such a status and level where the Awaited Saviour (ajt) was to convey his greetings to us, we would not remain in our state. We would roam around the world in pleasure and happiness, feeling honoured that among millions of people, we have received the special attention of God's proof on His earth. It is therefore worthy for us to put effort towards reaching this level of great success.

Then imagine what level and station a person would be if they are to receive God's greetings. It would, then, be incumbent on the worshipper, while supplicating to God, to say from within the depth of his existence:

اَللَّهُمَّ إِلَيْكَ تَوَجَّهْتُ وَرِضَاكَ طَلَبْتُ وَثَوَابَكَ اِبْتَغَيْتُ
وَبِكَ آمَنْتُ وَعَلَيْكَ تَوَكَّلْتُ

O God, to You I am turning my attention, it is Your contentment I am requesting, Your reward I want, as I believe in You and rely on You.[16]

4. Intercession of the Ahlul Bayt (ʿa)

If we want Almighty God to pay more attention and concern to us, it is necessary prior to commencing prayer to implore the Ahlul Bayt (ʿa), making them as our mediums to God. This kind of medium has been mentioned in the supplications before prayer, with emphasis given on reciting them. For example, in one of the signed statements issued by our Awaited Saviour, Imām al-Mahdī (ajt), it says:

---

16. *Biḥār al-Anwār*, vol. 81, p. 365. This supplication is to be recited when preparing to pray and facing the qiblah.

اَللَّهُمَّ صَلِّ عَلَى مُحَمَّدٍ وَآلِهِ وَصِلْنِي بِهِمْ وَلاَ تَقْطَعْنِي، اَللَّهُمَّ بِحُجَّتِكَ اِعْصِمْنِي، وَسَلاَمُكَ عَلَى آلِ يس مَوْلاَيَ، أَنْتَ اَلْجَاهُ عِنْدَ اَللَّهِ رَبِّكَ وَرَبِّي

O God, send Your salutations upon Muhammad and his Progeny, connect me to them and do not cut me [from them]. O God, protect me through Your proof (*ḥujjah*), and Your greetings upon the progeny of Yāsīn. O Master, you are glorified by your Lord and my Lord.[17]

In this same signed statement, it also says:

اَلسَّلاَمُ عَلَيْكُمْ أَنْتُمْ نُورُنَا، وَأَنْتُمْ جَاهُنَا أَوْقَاتَ صَلَوَاتِنَا، وَعِصْمَتُنَا لِدُعَائِنَا وَصَلاَتِنَا، وَصِيَامِنَا وَاسْتِغْفَارِنَا، وَسَائِرِ أَعْمَالِنَا

Greetings upon you [the Ahlul Bayt]. You are our light, you are our glory at times of our prayer, our immunity for our supplications, prayers, fasting, seeking forgiveness and all our other actions.[18]

As you can see in this noble letter, our Infallible Imāms (ʿa) and the Imām of our Time (ajt) have been mentioned as mediums between us and Almighty God, so much that acceptance of our actions, like our prayer, is by grace of their care, their attention and their intercession.

We are not worthy of appearing before God and pleading with Him due to our flaws and vices, but the Almighty established a way for us to follow in order to get close to Him, and this path is the Ahlul Bayt (ʿa). By turning to, and pleading with these holy lights, God will provide us

17. Ibid. vol. 91, p. 36. This supplication is called Duʿā Āl Yāsīn.
18. Ibid.

the blessings of His attention and provide for us. Turning to the Ahlul Bayt (ʿa) will grant us closeness to God and assist us in performing our prayers with a deeper heart. Indeed, intercession (*tawassul*) to God's vicegerents will keep Satan away from the vicinity of our hearts. With all our sins, our shortcomings and our transgressions that we commit towards God, *tawassul* to the Ahlul Bayt (ʿa) will result in the Almighty God forgiving our sins and sending down His blessings and success upon us. This is because they hold such a lofty status with God which leads to them interceding on our behalf.

We read in the following supplication attributed to the holy Prophet (ṣ):

اَللَّهُمَّ إِنِّي أَتَوَجَّهُ إِلَيْكَ بِمُحَمَّدٍ وآلِ مُحَمَّدٍ وأَتَقَرَّبُ بِهِمْ
إِلَيْكَ وَ أُقَدِّمُهُمْ بَيْنَ يَدَيْ حَوَائِجِي

O God, I turn to You through Muḥammad and his Progeny,
I get close to You through them and I place them in front of
me for my needs.[19]

We must pay attention to the holy Infallibles and vicegerents who are among the greatest of God's bounties upon us, as following them and with the blessings of their existence we can get closer to Almighty God.

In this era as well, the greatest divine blessing we have is the honourable and sacred presence of the Imam of our time (ajt), who is at the peak of nobility and honour. The more recognition we have of our living Imam's luminance and status, and the more we strive to please him and get closer to him, through him we will be able to gain closeness to the infinite realm of Almighty God.

---

19. *Biḥār al-Anwār*, v. 82, p. 177.

In fact, we must remember that everything comes from God and that nobody has anything of their own. We would not be able to pray if it weren't for God giving us strength, perception, and awareness. Paying attention to and understanding such essential monotheistic ideas would undoubtedly improve the efficacy and worth of prayer as well as play a significant part in elevating our spirituality.

The supplication says:

أَنْتَ مَنَنْتَ عَلَيَّ بِمَعْرِفَتِهِمْ فَاخْتِمْ لِي بِطَاعَتِهِمْ وَمَعْرِفَتِهِمْ وَ وَلاَيَتِهِمْ فَإِنَّهَا اَلسَّعَادَةُ وَاِخْتِمْ لِي بِهَا فإنك عَلىٰ كُلِّ شَيْءٍ قَدِيرٌ

You favoured me in recognising them, so complete me with obeying them, knowing them well and following them, for indeed this is blissful. Keep me on this path till the end of my life, as You have power over all things.[20]

20. *Al-Kāfī*, v. 2, p. 544. *Biḥār al-Anwār*, v. 81, p. 370.

Chapter Two
Sincerity in Prayer

The Status of Sincerity in Prayer

The lowest level of intention in prayer, without which, prayer will be invalid is that the person praying does so in obedience to God's command. The motive for this person praying is that they must obey God's command, and if God had not mandated prayer, or such an act had not been required by God, they would not have prayed. On such a level and motivation, a person's prayer would be valid and they have fulfilled their obligation, without a need to repeat it or redo it. As for a prayer to be accepted by Almighty God, the prayer must be performed sincerely and purely for the sake of gaining closeness to Almighty God. Such a prayer will bring about spiritual development and perfection, bringing the worshipper closer to God. As explained, some narrations mention that acts of worship and the related intention behind them can be divided into three types:

1. Worship of slaves: this is worship performed out of fear of God's punishment.

2. Worship of merchants: this is worship performed with hope of attaining rewards and Heaven.
3. Worship of the free: this worship is purely for God alone.

The highest level of sincerity, which is pure flawless sincerity to God with no motive or request for oneself, is indeed true, but it is a vast station that one must reach by travelling a long and challenging route.

Those who worship God out of fear of His punishment or greed for His heaven will not reach complete sincerity, and the grade of their sincerity is mixed with self-love and self-interests. We regularly witness how encouragement, threats and admonishing of average people affect them, especially the young who have just reached the age of becoming religiously responsible, making them pray, to the extent that if these encouragements or threats would not be there, they would not pray.

In reality however, one must travel a very long journey to reach that stage of sincerity where the self is disregarded and this person is completely annihilated in God's majesty.

ʿAllāmah al-Majlisī on Gaining Closeness to God in Prayer

On the difficulty of acquiring sincerity in prayer, ʿAllāmah Muḥammad Bāqir al-Majlisī (1037/1628 – 1110/1699 AH/CE) says:

> As for the intention of gaining closeness (*al-qurbah*), this is the most difficult of things and cannot be achieved when wanting to perform prayers. Rather, acquiring the [sincere] intention of wanting to gain closeness to God is dependent on great struggles, correct mindset, and removing

love of this world, wealth and worldly statuses from one's self... In all these stages one must beseech the Almighty to grant them this disposition and potential and to be granted success and guidance from Him. Each person acts according to their own disposition, and each person's intention is subject to what is in their heart: love of God, love of this world, love of status, love of money, or anything else. Of course, eradicating the roots of these symptoms from the self is extremely difficult and challenging, correcting one's intention is close to impossible. This is why the Prophetic narration says:

نِيَّةُ ٱلْمُؤْمِنِ خَيْرٌ مِنْ عَمَلِهِ .

The intention of a believer is better than his act.[21]

How many worshippers who are attached to this world and think their intention is purely for God, but in their whole life they were worshipping nothing but their self (*nafs*) and their desire (*hawā*).[22]

Scholars of Akhlāq have discussed in detail the topic of intention and sincerity in their books, especially in books like *Asrār al-Ṣalāt*, by Imām Khomeini,[23] and books written by al-Shahīd al-Thānī (911/1506 – 966/1559 AH/CE)[24] and Mirzā Jawād Āghā Malakī Tabrīzī (1274/1857

---

21. *'Awālī al-La'ālī*, v. 1, p. 406.
22. *Biḥār al-Anwār*, v. 18, p. 372.
23. The late Imām Khomeini wrote two profoundly spiritual books on prayer, and they are: *Sirr Asrār al-Ṣalāt:-Ṣalāt al-'Ārifīn wa Mi'rāj al-Sālikīn* and *Ādāb al-Ṣalāt*.
24. His full name was Zayn al-Dīn ibn Nūr al-Dīn 'Alī ibn Aḥmad al-'Āmilī al-Jubā'ī, and the name of his book is *Asrār al-Ṣalāt*.

– 1925/1343 AH/CE).[25] There is also valuable information that must be read in the writings of Mullā Muḥammad Mahdī al-Narāqī (1128/1716 – 1209/1795 AH/CE) and his son Mullā Aḥmad al-Narāqī (1185/1771 – 1245/1829 AH/CE).[26] Of course, in this field it could be said that the famous book *Iḥyā' 'Ulūm al-Dīn* authored by Abū Ḥāmid al-Ghazālī (450/1058 – 505/1111 AH/CE) preceded all other books in this field. Al-Ghazālī explained these topics so masterfully.

Fortunately, one of our great scholars, Mullā Muḥsin al-Fayḍ al-Kāshānī (1007/1598 – 1091/1680 AH/CE) expanded and revised al-Ghazālī's *Iḥyā' 'Ulūm al-Dīn* in his book *al-Maḥajjah al-Bayḍā'*. Al-Fayḍ al-Kāshānī replaced the weak or problematic narrations al-Ghazālī used from Sunni sources in his *Iḥyā' al-'Ulūm* with narrations from the Ahlul Bayt ('a). This was how al-Fayḍ al-Kāshānī added value and merit to the book. In volume eight of *al-Maḥajjah al-Bayḍā'*, among the very important topics al-Fayḍ discusses is the topic of intention and sincerity. I recommend everyone to read these discussions, as they are very valuable and rare to find as well. It could be claimed that whatever others have written in this field have not really added anything more to what is in this book, but rather used it as reference and summarised it.

Showing Off Nullifies Prayer

There are certain things that completely nullify an act of worship and invalidate it. Not only will it remove any positive effect from the act of worship, but could also lead to one's plight. Showing off (*al-riyā'*) is considered one of the most important obstacles that hinder the effect of acts of worship and it is also the most common.

---

25. The name of his book was also *Asrār al-Ṣalāt*.
26. The books respectively to be mentioned here by them on this topic are *Jāmi' al-Sa'ādāt* and *Mi'rāj al-Sa'ādah*.

In this context, showing off means to pretend to be more attentive in front of others. This means to do something for the purpose of others to see them and praise and commend them. This person feels pleasure from such praise and becomes happy and proud. Whoever performs an act of worship with such an attention will be attempting to please others and are not attentive to whether this pleases God.

There are two verses in the Quran that mention showing-off in prayer. In the first verse, the Almighty says:

﴿فَوَيْلٌ لِلْمُصَلِّينَ ۝ الَّذِينَ هُمْ عَنْ صَلَاتِهِمْ سَاهُونَ ۝ الَّذِينَ هُمْ يُرَاءُونَ﴾

Woe to them who pray, —those who are heedless of their prayers, those who show off.[27]

And in the second verse:

﴿إِنَّ الْمُنَافِقِينَ يُخَادِعُونَ اللَّهَ وَهُوَ خَادِعُهُمْ وَإِذَا قَامُوا إِلَى الصَّلَاةِ قَامُوا كُسَالَىٰ يُرَاءُونَ النَّاسَ وَلَا يَذْكُرُونَ اللَّهَ إِلَّا قَلِيلًا﴾

The hypocrites indeed seek to deceive Allah, but it is He who outwits them. When they stand up for prayer, they stand up lazily, showing off to the people and not remembering Allah except a little.[28]

It is not just that this prayer will not benefit them at all, but also that they will be punished for it as well.[29]

---

27. Quran, 107:4–6.
28. Quran, 4:142.
29. The Holy Quran also referred to showing off in charity giving, in zakāt and in jihād as well. On showing off in zakāt, the Almighty says:

The opposite of showing off is sincerity, and sincerity means to perform something for the sake of adhering to divine command and acquiring God's content, and no other motive must be involved in this. A sincere person does not want to show his deeds or acts to other people for the purpose of gaining praise and commendation, but only seeks Almighty God.

Of course, is it possible that one's acts are done in the presence of others, but his intention is not for others to see him. It could be said that performing acts in front of others in certain circumstances is something recommended and an additional act of worship, as long as their intention is sincere and the act is done purely for the sake of God. We can see what Almighty God says about this in the Holy Quran in the case of charity giving:

﴿قُـل لِعِبـادِيَ الَّذيـنَ آمَنـوا يُقيمُـوا الـصَّلاةَ وَيُنفِقـوا مِمّـا رَزَقناهُـم سِرًّا وَعَلانِيَـةً﴾

Tell My servants who have faith to maintain the prayer and to spend out of what We have provided them with, secretly andopenly.[30]

There are numerous narrations that speak about concealing one's giving of charity and not allowing others to know about what one

---

﴿وَالَّذينَ يُنفِقونَ أَموالَهُم رِئاءَ النّاسِ وَلا يُؤمِنونَ بِاللَّهِ وَلا بِاليَومِ الآخِرِ﴾

And those who spend their wealth to be seen by people, and believe neither in Allah nor in the Last Day. [Quran, 4:38]

On showing off in jihād, the Almighty says:

﴿وَلا تَكونوا كَالَّذينَ خَرَجوا مِن دِيارِهِم بَطَرًا وَرِئاءَ النّاسِ﴾

Do not be like those who left their homes vainly and to show off to the people. [Quran, 8:47]

Therefore, showing off is not something just related to prayer alone, but any act of worship someone does for the sake of acting or showing to people is considered a *riyā'* worship.

30. Quran, 14:31.

is giving. One narration says that Almighty God would love it if His servants were to pay charity, his left hand should not know what his right hand would give away. Such narrations came to stress on how good it is to conceal giving for God (*infāq*), but nonetheless public giving could also be good at times. This is why the Quran and narrations have mentioned concealed and secret spending, and also public open spending. Public giving out is for the sake of inviting others to do it and encourage such a good deed. When we give charity in front of others for the sake of them learning from us, they get encouraged to do such righteous deeds as well. Of course, in these circumstances one must be very careful they do not fall into showing off or having pride, or else it will ruin their deed. There is a very fine boundary between giving away and spending for the sake of reminding others and to get their praises, and if someone is not cautious about this their spending might become showing off.

Because of this, we need to pay extra close attention to this matter and maintain strict self-control so that we don't live our lives thinking that we have correctly completed our prayers. Otherwise, with our hearts assured of it, we may only hear the following when our book of deeds is opened and we are being judged: "You were praying all these prayers for the sake of people, so go and take your reward from them!" One anecdote about how subtle showing off can be is that even angels cannot perceive it and that only Almighty God is aware of it.

The acts we do must go through numerous checkpoints before it reaches the level of acceptance. There is a narration that says a servant will perform an act, and it will elevate until it reaches the first heaven, and the angels appointed for that level to inspect the deeds. If they find no problem with it and accept it, it will go up to the second level. If angels in the second level don't find any problem with it, it will go up, until it gets to the seventh heaven. Although it has gone through numerous inspections, seven times, with each inspection more thorough than the other, and nothing seemingly wrong or bad in it, but when it reaches the presence of Almighty God, He will say: this servant has not done this for me, so he will have my curse.[31]

There are many more of such narrations which I fear if they are all narrated here one will reach some level of hopelessness. I repeat again that if one is not cautious and observant, they might fall into the trap of showing off.

Showing Off

We have explained that although any act can be performed to obtain God's contentment and can be considered as an act of worship, there are actions that must be done with the intention of gaining closeness to God and obeying the divine command. If such actions are not done with this intention, it will not only carry no reward, but could also lead to punishment. In these actions, which are considered as acts of worship in the specific sense, intention is the primary condition for the act to be valid. As a result, if the intention is wrong, the act of worship will be invalid. Even though our discussion has focused on prayer particularly, we have also mentioned other forms of worship that are also founded on intention; if one were to practise them with the intent of bragging, those forms of devotion would also be invalid.

There are discussions among jurists related to whether some acts of worship like *khums* and *zakāt* need to have intention of gaining closeness to God for it to be valid and accepted as being paid, or if it is accepted, but without the intention of *qurbah* he is considered as sinning because he did it for showing off, or showing off in giving *khums* and *zakāt* does not render the acts invalid or sinful, but causes

31. This is taken from a long narration in *Biḥār al-Anwār*, v. 67, pp. 246–247.

a loss of reward. These specialised discussions are related to jurists and outside the scope of our current discussion.

Actions that can be done as acts of worship and have intention of gaining closeness to God can be divided into two universal groups:

The first group are actions in which their primary essence is nothing other than showing servitude to Almighty God and nothing else, like prayer, fasting and hajj. The second group are actions in which their primary essence is not to just show servitude, but rather requires the intention of *qurbah* as its condition. For example, the primary purpose of legislating *zakāt* is to help the poor and the needy along with everything else zakāt is used for, but at the same time the intention of *qurbah* has also been considered when performing it. The late Imam Khomeini refers to this as "acts of closeness" (*al-afʿāl al-qurbiyya*).

In such a case where the essence of the action is showing servitude in front of God, the act must be done with sincere intention for the Almighty and cannot have any other intention. Therefore, if someone were to pray in one respect with the intention of keeping God's command, but also with the intent of boasting and receiving acclaim from others, their prayer would not only be invalid but also sinful. However, there are cases like giving away (*infāq*) where its essence is not to show servitude. This means if one does not have the intention of *qurbah* when giving, its effect will just be in that limit and it will have no further benefit for the person doing it, but it also does not necessitate punishment. The person spending in this situation will be like someone throwing their money in the ocean.[32] The benefit and effectiveness of this type of act lies in performing it with the intention

32. Of course, doing so as far as engaging in wasting (*isrāf*) would be considered as a sin and publishable, but does not necessitate punishment just because he does not give away.

of gaining closeness to God, which means intention of closeness is the foundation of the action, and without it the act will have no title for it to have an effect. As the Quran says, the act must have:

﴿يُرِيدُونَ وَجْهَهُ﴾

Desiring only Him.[33]

And:

﴿إِلَّا ابْتِغَاءَ وَجْهِ رَبِّهِ الْأَعْلَىٰ﴾

But seeks only the pleasure of his Lord, the Most Exalted.[34]

In any case, if we want any act to take a form of worshipping, then it must be done with sincerity and for the sake of gaining closeness to Almighty God. To complete this discussion, reference will be made to a few narrations:

It is said in the following *ḥadīth qudsī*, narrated from Imām al-Ṣādiq (a) that Almighty God said:

أَنَا خَيْرُ شَرِيكٍ فَمَنْ عَمِلَ لِي وَلِغَيْرِي فَهُوَ لِمَنْ عَمِلَهُ غَيْرِي

I am the best partner, so whoever does something for Me and for someone other than Me, then what they did is for someone other than Me.[35]

Each and every individual who takes part in a specific act will gain a portion of a return or profit from it. Almighty God says I am the

33. Quran, 6:52.
34. Quran, 92:20.
35. *Biḥār al-Anwār*, v. 69, p. 299, h. 32.

best partner, and that is because I forgo the complete portion of my share, as large as it may be, and I give it to My partner. If prayer was performed, and 99% was for God and 1% was for people, God will forgo His portion of 99% and give it to the people so that the whole prayer is for them. This means that any act of worship that has even the least portion for other than God, one will be inflicted with such a fate that God will reject the entire thing. At times, this rejection will be just the act being invalid and having no reward, and at other times, in addition to that, there will also be punishment.[36]

Signs of Sincerity and Showing Off (Feigning Virtuousness)

There are different ways and signs of defining if an action one is doing is sincere or not. If one was to look into these ways and signs, it will become very clear for them if their intention in what they are doing is sincere or not.

If someone was to build a hospital, they must see how they would react if someone else's name was written on the hospital instead of their name. Would it annoy them or not? If the act was for God, it should have no difference for the person whether their name is written or not, and if someone was to feel otherwise then this serves as evidence that their act was not really sincere. Showing off is sometimes hidden from the person himself, as he assumes that his deed is sincere, whereas in reality that is not the case. Among the

---

36. It must be noted that intention is not something that can easily be amended, as it needs preliminaries. It is not that whatever someone wants to do, at any time and with any intention, they can do it. In order for intention to become sincere, prior to that there are preliminary steps that must be taken, like recognition (*maʿrifa*), faith (*īmān*) and attention (*tawajjuh*).

duties of scholars of *Akhlāq* is to aim at informing people of what their hidden unseen motives are in their behaviour and actions, to which they might not generally be paying attention.

For example, if someone was to pray in a mosque and in congregation, he must see if other people had not come to the mosque and he was all alone, would he be praying the exact same way? If the answer is no, then he knows that *riyā'* has found its way to his prayer. If it was dark and nobody was able to see his movements or his face and what he is doing during his prayer, would he be doing it the same way now that there is light and others can see him? If the answer is no, this is a sign that his deeds are accompanied with *riyā'*. If he was to always pray in a specific place in the mosque, and then one day he was not able to pray in that same regular place, would this annoy him? If he is annoyed, then this is a sign that his deed is not sincere, and it might be that the place where the act is being done also influences his act.

If the person is an imam of congregational prayer and makes a mistake in his prayer, which makes him feel embarrassed and start to sweat - this is a sign that the presence or absence of people strongly influences him. If there were no people, he would not be shy because of his mistake, but because there are people around him, he is embarrassed, and this is also a level of *riyā'*.

Another example is if someone was to go every day to the mosque with his friend, and one day his friend was busy and was not able to go, so this person did not go. This obviously means that his intention was not sincere in the previous days, and that having his friend go with him was a part of his intention.

Regarding this very example, the late Mirzā Jawād Āghā Malakī Tabrīzī mentions the following story in his book *Asrār al-Ṣalāt*:

A distinguished person for years prayed behind an eminent scholar and would always pray in a specific place in the first row. One day, when he got to the prayer, the first row was full and he was not able to pray in the first row, nor in the place where he regularly stands. He was forced to pray in another place and during prayer felt ashamed that he was praying in that row and that particular place - because people always saw him in the first row - and now he is, for example, praying in the second row. This made him feel embarrassed.

Mirzā Jawād Āghā Malakī Tabrīzī narrates that this man re-performed all his prayers that he had been praying in this state for the last thirty years. He says until now I did not know that I was praying for others to see me in the first row, and now I am embarrassed to stand in the second row. I now understand that my intention was not sincere, and there was something else involved other than God. If my intention was purely for the sake of God, there should be no difference for me between praying in the first row or the second row. For me, the first row or second row should have no difference at all.[37]

Another story that Mirzā Jawād Āghā Malakī Tabrīzī narrates in this book is:

During the days of Muḥarram, someone always wanted to participate in a specific place for mourning (*majlis 'azā'*). One day he felt that this particular majlis was important for him, so he thought to himself and asked: If I went to participate in a mourning ceremony to cry for Imām Ḥusain and uphold the rituals of the Master of martyrs (a), then from this perspective, none of the majālis are different to each other, so why do I always want to come to this specific majlis?

He thought about this for a while until finally after serious contemplation he understood why this majlis is special for him and

---

37. See: *Asrār al-Ṣalāt*

why he preferred it to others, and he then decided that from then onwards he would participate in the majālis that do not have any specific preference for him.

Hidden Showing Off

If a worship is sincere, its value will be at such a level that at times even angels cannot define how valuable it is, and only Almighty God is capable of evaluating its reward. However, if the intention for an act of worship is not sincere, then this act is like fake merchandise that has no real value. It is like poisoned food that not only has no value but could also be harmful or even lethal. In Islamic rulings, if one drop of blood the size of a needle-head was to drop into a very large container of liquid food or drink, that whole container of juice or food would become contaminated and impure. The whole contents of the container must be disposed of and thrown away, even though so much effort and money was spent in preparing it.

Some of our acts of worship could at times be similar to this. We could perform a certain act of worship with so many difficulties, but because we carried motives other than God, even a very small percentage, the whole action could be lost and wasted. According to narrations, Almighty God will address His angels and command them to throw this deed back at its owner's face.[38]

Therefore, in addition to the act of worship and making sure we observe its rulings and conduct it in its correct form, we must also pay attention to the intention. God forbid, after a period of time we may come to realise that our intentions were not sincere and for all this time our acts of worship had no benefit for us.

---

38. See: *Biḥār al-Anwār*, v. 67, pp. 246–247.

There is a narration that has been mentioned in Shīʿa and Sunni sources that after the Prophet (s) considered *riyā'* a type of polytheism (*shirk*), he said:

إِنَّ اَلشِّرْكَ أَخْفَى مِنْ دَبِيبِ اَلنَّمْلِ عَلَى صَفَاةٍ سَوْدَاءَ فِي لَيْلَةٍ ظَلْمَاءَ

Polytheism is more hidden than the creeping of an ant on a black rock on a dark night.[39]

An ant is a very small insect, without long hands or legs, and the rock could be soft and slippery, so when the ant moves over the rock there is no friction or sticking, and therefore no noise is made that a human can hear. This crawling on a dark night will be hidden from all aspects and cannot be felt or perceived in any way. The holy Prophet (s) says that polytheism infiltrates into the human being's heart so inconspicuously concealed, even more than this creeping. Therefore, showing off, which is a kind of polytheism, can be like this imperceptible act and it could be that the following verse refers to this as well:

﴿وَما يُؤمِنُ أَكثَرُهُم بِاللَّهِ إِلّا وَهُم مُشرِكونَ﴾

And most of them do not believe in Allah without ascribing partners to Him.[40]

Of course, polytheism has various situations and levels, and we must request from God and strive to fulfil our worshipping of Him away from any level of polytheism, showing off or any non-Divine motives.

In some acts of worship, it is easier to distinguish *riyā'* from non-*riyā'*, and there are clearer signs for it. One case for this is what we as

---

39. Al-Ḥurr al-ʿĀmilī, *Wasā'il al-Shīʿah*, v. 16, ch. 36, p. 254, h. 21501.
40. Quran, 12:106.

students of religious sciences do in our propagating and ascending the pulpit. Without doubt, guiding and educating people and spreading God's religion or explaining Islamic teachings and laws are all considered as among the greatest acts of worship. Addressing Imām ʿAlī (s), the holy Prophet (s) said:

لَأَنْ يَهْدِيَ اَللّٰهُ بِكَ رَجُلاً وَاحِداً خَيْرٌ لَكَ مِمَّا طَلَعَتْ عَلَيْهِ اَلشَّمْسُ

If through God you were to guide another person, this would be greater for you than whatever the sun rises over.[41]

Guiding people is therefore so virtuous that it is beyond description and its reward cannot even be imagined. However, this act itself with all its reward, if it is not for God, will hold no value whatsoever. The reward will be for the propagation, lecturing and guiding people only if it is done to please God, but how do we know if what we are doing is for God or not? One way of understanding this is to see if there was another propagator or lecturer who says the same thing and what he says results in someone being guided, would we genuinely be equally happy, or would we be happy and feel pleased only because we accomplished this act? If our goal is to guide people, we should not be feeling in any way different between the two cases.

If you were to build a hospital where people go for treatment, and this hospital treats poor patients free of charge - you will get the reward whether the hospital has your name on it or someone else's name. If your goal was to please God alone, you will achieve it whether your name is there or not. If on the other hand you insist on having your name on the hospital, then you must not doubt that you do not have sincerity in your intention.

41. *Biḥār al-Anwār*, v. 32, p. 448, h. 394.

Of course, reaching such a level of sincerity is not easy as it needs a lot of work and effort, resulting in gaining value for actions performed with difficulty, due to the great difference between a sincere act and a non-sincere act.

A Story about Showing Off and Sincerity

There is a story about Allāmah al-Majlisī, and I am not certain about its authenticity, but nonetheless it does have a practical lesson, even if it did not really occur in this particular way. It is said that after the passing away of Allāmah al-Majlisī, someone saw him in his dream and asked him: What was it that saved you - from all the services you gave, all the books you wrote, and all the lessons you taught, what was that which was most useful for you? Allāmah al-Majlisī replied: "None of these things I did had as much use as I expected, because for each of them there were some faults and defects."

So, he was asked what it was that saved him, and he said: One day I was walking in a street while holding an apple, and there was a woman (it seems she was a Jewish woman) walking with her son in her arms, and the child happened to see the apple in my hand. From how the young boy reacted, I understood that he wanted to take the apple from my hand, so when the mother saw him, she prevented him and grabbed his hand. I then went forward and gave the apple to the young boy to make him happy. Now, in this realm, I am being told that the only deed I did that was 100% sincere is this deed, as it had no level of flattering a ruler or wanting fame, or showing off, or anything else. I gave him that apple purely to please God and to bring happiness to that young boy.

What is important for God is sincerity and purity. Almighty God wants His servants to deal with Him free of any spite or deception.

God will not accept anything unless it is purely for Him. He says He is the best partner, and He will forfeit His share to the other partner who was joined with Him in their deeds.[42] God does not take into consideration how great or small a deed is. What matters is the motivation behind the action. The aim of an action is reflected in its spirit, and we must increase our understanding of and devotion to God to the point where sincerity and purity are produced naturally. We should not get happy and say we have worshipped God and avoided sin, because maybe in that act of worship or avoidance of sin, we might have extended our sight to other than God. We might have wanted other people to praise us, or to be famously known as ascetic, pious, etc. If our deeds are not solely for God, their account rests with those for whom they were performed.

42. See: *Biḥār al-Anwār*, v. 69, p. 299, h. 32.

Chapter Three
The Spirit of Prayer

The Real Prayer

As explained, we understand from what Islam teaches us that the most important and best of actions in God's eyes to please Him and gain closeness to Him is "prayer". The Quran and narrations explain the benefits and effects of prayer, regarding it the greatest and loftiest of deeds. Our sacred shari'a explicitly refers to prayer as the "greatest deed" (*khayr al-ʿamal*), and we confess to this in the adhan and *iqāmah* of our five daily prayers. Among the specialities and benefits of prayer is:

اَلصَّلاَةِ مِعْرَاجُ اَلْمُؤْمِنِ.

Prayer is the ascension of the believer.[43]

43. *Biḥār al-Anwār*, v. 79, p. 303, ḥ. 2. According to our scholars, this tradition attributed to the Prophet (s) is in fact not a narration, but rather a statement inspired by narrations related to the story of the Prophetic Nocturnal Ascension

With all this said, unfortunately we still rarely benefit from our prayer in its proper way. We do not feel the pleasure of prayer that we perform, and we do not feel its effects and results in our existence. It is rather the opposite, prayer for us is mostly something heavy and a burden. We turn to prayer while hating it. When we finish our prayer, it is as if we have removed a heavy weight from our shoulders that was tiring us. All this and our prayer is usually no more than a few minutes, or not exceeding ten minutes, but this small time becomes so heavy for us, as though it is hours for us. Then when we finish this prayer, we take a long sigh of relief, as if we were a caged bird, and now released to fly freely. We just want to get to the end of the prayer, so we can go on with our daily affairs. This is how it has been expressed in the Holy Quran:

﴿وَإِنَّهَا لَكَبِيرَةٌ إِلَّا عَلَى الْخَاشِعِينَ﴾

And it [prayer] is indeed hard, except for the humble.[44]

Of course, regardless of any deficiencies in our prayers or their perceived lack of impact on us, it is infinitely superior to continue with them than to abandon them altogether. The very fact that someone fulfils their duty in these few minutes in the presence of their Lord and bows down to prostrate onto soil is itself something of very high value. However, what we are discussing is the value of prayer and its importance and the benefits that we can receive from prayer being much greater. The distance that separates us from our form of prayer and the real prayer and its effects is like zero to infinity.

We are very far away from that lofty angelic prayer, and we are unfortunately deprived of its astonishing effects. As previously explained, we are deprived because we have limited our prayer to

44. Quran, 2:45.

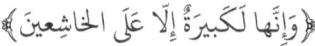

just the external words we utter and movements we do, with no attention to its spirit and reality. Someone praying and not paying attention to its meanings and its movements is similar to a fortune-teller or an astrologist who repeats peculiar sentences which they do not understand, nor does anyone else. It cannot be expected that a prayer based on lip-synching and going up and down lead its owner to an ascension. The prayer of most of us resembles this prayer. We just perform it, and in reality, at times our prayer is no different to a demonstration, where we demonstrate prayer, but not the prayer itself.

Prayer does not necessarily need to be long. It can be short and brief, but its spirit could create miracles and the person praying could elevate from the lowest of low to the highest peak of nobility and majesty. This is why we must strive and ask the Almighty to grant our prayer such a spirit, and if successful we will certainly witness its effects in actuality (as much as we perceive its spirit).

If a prayer gains its spirit, its effect will be avoiding immorality and vice, as the Almighty says in the Holy Quran:

﴿إِنَّ الصَّلَاةَ تَنْهَىٰ عَنِ الْفَحْشَاءِ وَالْمُنكَرِ﴾

Indeed, the prayer prevents indecencies and wrongs.[45]

We see many people, however, who pray and immediately after leaving the mosque, pursue sinful activity. That prayer did not have an effect in preventing them from committing a sin and a bad act. How many people are there who upon finishing their prayer, they turn to a prohibited (*ḥarām*) gaze, or listen to *ḥarām*, or talk *ḥarām*, or engage in *ḥarām* transactions, or any other prohibited act?!

45. Quran, 29:45.

At times it could even happen that some do not even need to leave the mosque to perform such prohibited acts. They could even do it inside the mosque, like backbiting, slandering, lying and mocking others. We must really ask what kind of prayer did they just perform? Why doesn't this prayer prevent us from such sins?

Imām 'Alī (a) narrates that the holy Prophet (s) said to him:

> يَا عَلِيُّ، إِنَّمَا مَنْزِلَةُ اَلصَّلَوَاتِ اَلْخَمْسِ لِأُمَّتِي كَنَهَرٍ جَارٍ عَلَى بَابِ أَحَدِكُمْ، فَمَا ظَنُّ أَحَدِكُمْ لَوْ كَانَ فِي جَسَدِهِ دَرَنٌ ثُمَّ اِغْتَسَلَ فِي ذَلِكَ اَلنَّهَرِ خَمْسَ مَرَّاتٍ فِي اَلْيَوْمِ، أَكَانَ يَبْقَى فِي جَسَدِهِ دَرَنٌ؟ فَكَذَلِكَ وَاَللَّهِ اَلصَّلَوَاتُ اَلْخَمْسُ لِأُمَّتِي

> O 'Alī, the status of the five daily prayers in my ummah is like a running river at your doorstep. What would you expect if someone had dirt on their body and washed themselves in that river five times a day, would there be any dirt left on their body? By God, this is how the five prayers are for my ummah.[46]

Although we pray five times a day, we are still contaminated with the pollution and dirt of various sins. This is all because we are not truly praying, but rather what we do resembles prayer.

The question here is if we want our prayer to be real and carry that spirit, what do we need to do?

---

46. *Biḥār al-Anwār*, v. 79, p. 220, ḥ. 41.

Three Steps Towards Obtaining the Spirit and Reality of Prayer

We must take three steps to get closer to the spirit of prayer and benefit from its reality:

First step: To pay attention to the prayer while performing it. It frequently occurs that when one recites Sūrat-al-Fātiḥa and then starts to recite Sūrat al-Tawḥīd, they don't even remember how they commenced or finished Sūrat al-Fātiḥa. One could even reach the end of prayer and then realise that he was praying. This shows that he had no conscious attention to the prayer and what he was doing.[47]

Therefore, the first step is to get to the reality and spirit of prayer, which is "to pay attention to what we are doing". From the very beginning when we stand for *takbīratul-iḥrām*, and before we say *Allahu-akbar*, we must pay attention to why we are standing here and what we are about to do? Rather, more than that, we must become attentive from the first words in our adhan and *iqāmah*. The lowest level here is we will be like someone who memorises a script and wants to read it out to someone, paying attention to read it out correctly and not mix up the words or make a mistake. Of course, with repetition and after time, reciting prayer becomes a "disposition" (*malakah*), and one is able to have a weak level of attention or be half alert and still recite the prayer in its correct form, but this amount

47. There is no doubt that a human does have a level of attention while he/she is willingly performing such acts, because it would be impossible to do a willing act without any kind of attention. However, such willing acts need the least level of attention, and in relation to prayer, the point here is that weak attention that is so weak that when one is in the third *rak'ah*, they do not remember reciting the *tashahhud*. This kind of prayer misses the spirit, and a person praying this kind of a prayer will not achieve perfection or excel.

of attention is not enough for prayer to be accepted or to achieve its full effects.

Second Step: To perform the prayer that we will benefit from, we must pay attention to the meanings and purport of each sentence or invocation we say. This is something we must certainly persist in achieving. If we have not been successful in achieving it in our prayer, then in our next prayer, or in the prayer after. We must renew our determination to achieve it in our next prayer, and this is something imperative. The method to achieve this is prior to uttering any sentence we summon the meaning in our mind, and then recite the sentence. For example, when we want to say *Allahu-akbar*, we first summon the concept in our mind, that God is greater than everything and anything, and we then say *Allahu-akbar*. If we were to practise this, we will reach a level where we are able to always pay attention to the meanings and concepts of the words and sentences we utter with our tongues. This is of course a very important and fundamental issue, and if we were successful in doing this, we will be taking a major step towards achieving our goal.

Third step: By following this path, we hope to bring our words and our hearts closer together. While in prayer if we were to say *iyyāka naʿbudu wa iyyāka nastaʿīn* (You alone we worship and from You alone we seek assistance), our state of mind should also be such that our hearts seek assistance from God alone and nobody else. When we do the *takbīratul-iḥrām* and say *Allahu-akbar,* the belief in our heart should really be that "God is greater".

Do we truly and genuinely testify from the depth of our hearts and souls that God is greater than everything? Does this statement manifest and appear in our behaviour and our actions? If most of us were to think and contemplate on our state, we will see, God forbid, that we do not consider the presence of God to be equal to that of a child. Most of our actions we would even be ashamed to do so in front of a child but commit worse things with absolute audacity in front of Almighty God. On a practical and behavioural level, we don't consider God to be "greater" but rather "smaller" than everyone.

There are different levels of harmonising one's state in prayer with what flows from their tongue. There could be a level or levels that all are able to achieve through practice, and there are levels specific for God's saints who have reached lofty states of recognition and perfection. Our Infallible Imāms have astounding states in their prayer, as their attention in prayer was exclusively towards God and nothing else.

A Story from Imām 'Alī (a)

There is a famous story about the Commander of the faithful ('a) ,when he was wounded with an arrow in his foot, and those around him were not able to extract it from him. In those days there was no anaesthetics or medicine to relieve pain, which made removing the arrow a very difficult task. They waited until Imām 'Alī ('a) stood to pray, and while he was in prayer they pulled the arrow out of his foot without him noticing or feeling pain. Imagining such an event might be difficult for us, but this not only happened with Imām 'Alī ('a), but also with a student from the School of Imām 'Alī ('a).

A Story from Ayatullah al-Khwānsārī

I heard this story from very reliable individuals whom I trust and were eyewitnesses to the event. One day the great scholar Ayatullah Sayyid Aḥmad al-Khwānsārī (1309/1891–1405/1985 AH/CE) became sick, and this illness required him having stomach surgery. Naturally, it was required for him to go under anaesthesia so they could perform the procedure, but the grand Ayatullah al-Khwānsārī refused to be sedated for certain reasons,[48] and he requested that the operation be done without sedating him.

The physicians insisted on the importance of anaesthetising him, but he told them to go ahead without it. In the end, the doctors opened his stomach without giving him any anaesthetics, cut off the necessary portions, and then stitched him back up. Throughout this time, Ayatullah al-Khwānsārī did not express any reaction that might have indicated the least level of pain or disturbance. The doctors could not believe what had occurred in front of them.

It is said that this great scholar turned with his complete existence to Almighty God throughout the operation, and it was as if he was completely unaware of himself and the world around him. Without doubt, whoever can focus their concentration to this level during a surgical operation is able to achieve this level of attention in prayer. In any case, these things are achievable, and we must put enough effort and ask Almighty God to grant us such a state and rank.

The late Imam Khomeini and other scholars of Akhlāq always advise to "aim at instilling these realities into the heart". What does it mean by establishing words and meanings into the heart? In this regard, scholars want to distinguish between the "mind" (*al-dhihn*) and the "heart" (*al-qalb*). Fundamentally, the human mind is the position and place of concepts (*ma'ānī*). It is possible for a disbeliever to conceptualise the meaning of "*lā ilāha illā Allah*" in their mind, but why do they still stay a disbeliever? It is because the conceptualisation

48. It could be that being sedated and losing consciousness, like death, would have resulted in the nullifying of his verdicts, and as he was a Source of Emulation (Marjaʿ Taqlīd), he did not want it to cause problem for those who emulate him. (Ghiyathi Kermani).
My assumption is that losing consciousness nullifies any verbal wikālahs given to him or by him, which is why he was reluctant to be sedated.

of its meaning is done in their mind, but it is not affirmed in their heart. Therefore, a believer is a believer because, in addition to conceptualising its meaning in their mind, they also believe in it and affirm it in their heart. What Imam Khomeini and other scholars of Akhlāq have said stem from the Holy Quran, like the following verse:

﴿قالَتِ الأَعرابُ آمَنّا قُل لَم تُؤمِنوا وَلٰكِن قولوا
أَسلَمنا وَلَمّا يَدخُلِ الإيمانُ في قُلوبِكُم﴾

The desert Arabs say: We believe. Say (unto them, O Muhammad): You do not believe, but rather say "We submit," for the faith has not yet entered into your hearts.[49]

Some Bedouins would come to the Prophet (ṣ) and bear witness to the oneness of God and his prophecy, saying "*ashhadu an lā ilāha illā Allah wa ashhadu anna Muḥammad rasūllulah*". They thought that this was faith, and that is why they would just say we believe in God and His Prophet. Then this verse came down, saying to them that although they verbally confessed the testimony of faith and performed their duties, however faith had yet to enter into their hearts. This is because if it had entered the heart, its effects would appear in their actions and behaviour.

It is for this reason that we must aim at establishing the realities in what we utter in our prayer or what we show in practice in our behaviour into our hearts as well. If we say "You alone we worship and You alone we ask for help," we must believe it with our hearts, and we must not have any hope or belief in any help or assistance other than from God. If we show our reverence and humility in front of God, and we go down to prostrate, we must keep our heart and inner

49. Quran, 49:14.

side away from any form of I-ness and selfishness. In reality, we must be worshippers who have genuine pure submission to Almighty God.

A Fable or Real?

It is unfortunate that we are so far away from such matters, so far that we sometimes think these words are just fables or illusions and nothing else. We think that they are slogans chanted by people wandering in their own nature, but these matters are real and many of them explicitly mentioned in the Holy Quran and narrations from Ahlul Bayt. As far as I am concerned, when I pondered on the meaning of this verse for the first time, I was extremely astonished and I realised how far away we are from the Quran and its teachings. When the Almighty describes the believers, He says:

﴿إِذا يُتلىٰ عَلَيهِم يَخِرّونَ لِلأَذقانِ سُجَّدًا ۝ وَيَقولونَ
سُبحانَ رَبِّنا إِن كانَ وَعدُ رَبِّنا لَمَفعولًا ۝ وَيَخِرّونَ
لِلأَذقانِ يَبكونَ وَيَزيدُهُم خُشوعًا﴾

When it is recited to them, fall down in prostration on their faces. and say, "Immaculate is our Lord! Indeed Our Lord's promise is bound to be fulfilled." Weeping, they fall down on their faces, and it increases them in humility.[50]

Real believers and those in whose heart's faith has been implanted and fall to the ground and weep as the Quran is read to them. They don't learn how to do this, and it is a natural response to being influenced by the Quran. They become more deferential whenever the Quran is read to them. I have lived a long time and am over sixty years old, but I have never seen anyone react in such a way to hearing verses from the Holy Quran. Of course, I have witnessed individuals

50. Quran, 17:107–109.

cry as they listen to the Quran, but I have never witnessed anyone kneel on the ground, bury their face in the dirt, and weep.

Another verse similar to this above verse is:

﴿إِذا تُتلىٰ عَلَيهِم آياتُ الرَّحمٰنِ خَرّوا سُجَّدًا وَبُكِيًّا﴾

When the signs of the All-beneficent were recited to them, they would fall down weeping in prostration.[51]

For whom were these verses revealed? What aim is there in mentioning these states and descriptions of believers? Is it to inform us that there were believers who had such characteristics? Shouldn't it be that we aim to acquire such characteristics within ourselves? Should we not be able to at least see one person from among the believers around us who have such a state?

This itself shows how far we are away from the examples of the Quran and Sunna. In the past, there were numerous individuals who would be described as such, but these days with the increase of adornments and decorations of this world, and competing and fighting over materialist things, it has become very rare. It is seldom that we find people with such states.

In our current era, the situation has reached such a level where if someone does weep while crying or shed tears when listening to verses from the Quran, it would be considered as an innovation and what the person is doing is unjustifiable and meaningless. Can we regard what was clearly mentioned in the Quran as an innovation in religion? If the explicit Quranic verse is something other than religion, then what is religion, and if the Quran cannot define religion or the

51. Quran, 19:58.

characteristics of the believers, then how can one understand this important matter?

Almighty God wanting to explain to us the greatness of the meanings and teachings of the Quran says:

﴿لَو أَنزَلنا هٰذَا القُرآنَ عَلىٰ جَبَلٍ لَرَأَيتَهُ خاشِعًا مُتَصَدِّعًا مِن خَشيَةِ اللَّهِ﴾

Had We sent down this Qur'ān upon a mountain, you would have surely seen it humbled [and] go to pieces with the fear of Allah.[52]

If the Quran had descended on a mountain, the mountain would have disintegrated. However, most people's hearts have grown so hard that no Quranic verse can affect or change them. A heart that the Quran cannot affect in response to listening to the Quran is a heart harder than a stone. The Quran will not affect them in any way, and not change them at all. Indeed, we say: what has occurred that we have become so cold and soulless towards divine verses? Has the time not come to reassess the state of our heart and spirit so that hopefully we can at least feel the delight of remembering God and His verses:

﴿أَلَم يَأنِ لِلَّذينَ آمَنوا أَن تَخشَعَ قُلوبُهُم لِذِكرِ اللَّهِ وَما نَزَلَ مِنَ الحَقِّ وَلا يَكونوا كَالَّذينَ أوتُوا الكِتابَ مِن قَبلُ فَطالَ عَلَيهِمُ الأَمَدُ فَقَسَت قُلوبُهُم﴾

Is it not time yet for those who have faith that their hearts should be humbled for Allah's remembrance and to the truth which has come down [to them], and to be not like

52. Quran, 59:21.

those who were given the Book before? Time took its toll on them and so their hearts were hardened.[53]

Has the time not come for believers to adopt a humble attitude so they do not become like those whose hearts start to harden, where their eyes cannot produce not even one teardrop? Is it not time for leaving this state of rigidness and coldness that the heart is suffering? How many people have had hearts and souls melt from listening to verses from the Quran, and return to repent to God, so why can't we be like them?

There is a famous story about the highway robber al-Fuḍayl ibn 'Iyāḍ (d. 187 AH/803 CE).[54] One night while preparing his criminal ways, he climbed a wall, and coincidently heard a person in the house recite the verse: "*Is it not time yet....*"[55] Hearing this verse created tremors deep in his heart, and it completely turned him around. He immediately repented and said: "Yes, the time has come." Al-Fuḍayl changed because of this verse, so much that he became one of God's saints. Indeed, has it not come the time for the teachings and meanings of the words and invocations of prayer that we utter with our tongues to correspond to what we have in our mind and enter into our hearts? Has the time not come for our hearts to be more present in prayer, and we not be that careless? Our hope is that the Almighty gives us the success to change us onto this path.

---

53. Quran, 57:16.
54. al-Fuḍayl ibn 'Iyāḍ (107–187 AH) was a bandit who would raid caravans and rob travellers in Khurasan and Syria, but yet he still prayed and performed other acts of worship. Upon hearing this verse, he completely transformed, leaving his criminal ways and becoming a very pious person.
55. Quran, 57:16.

Methods to Achieve Presence of the Heart in Prayer

a) Contemplating on the Benefits of Presence of the Heart in Prayer

One available method of solving this problem is thinking and pondering on the benefits of attention and presence of the heart in prayer, and also the harms of neglecting it. If someone was to believe in the benefit of any act and perceive how harmful it is to leave it, they will strive to do it and take concern in observing it. The reality is we do not believe or trust the benefits of prayer and the detriments that result from not paying attention to it.

Due to the limitations of the mind, comparing this to a business transaction will somehow make it more understandable. Consider a businessman who wants to do two transactions with a certain amount of funds. The first transaction will result in about 1 million dollars, and the second transaction will generate 1 billion dollars in profit. If the businessman chooses the transaction that profits 1 million dollars, how much loss will he incur to himself and how much will he lose after that?

Of course, we have previously mentioned the difference between an attentive prayer and a prayer without attention, being beyond any number or calculation, but if we wanted to just explain the difference as far as numbers, it would be similar to this. It is as if we are able to gain 100 billion dollars within five minutes with our prayer, but we have sufficed only with one hundred dollars. Is there a loss greater than this?

Another example: with five minutes of prayer, we are able to obtain millions of dollars worth of diamonds and pearls, but we are content with glass that has absolutely no value! Now that we want to say "*Allahu-akbar*" to commence the prayer both paths are open in front of us. We have this choice every day, or rather numerous times every day, but we replace our prayer with that piece of glass or an amount of money that is worthless.

If we were to think about this prior to any prayer, that the reward of our prayer could be a precious gem which no jeweller could estimate how valuable it is, then we might come back to our senses and not sell our prayer for such a cheap price. If we were to understand the real value of our prayer, we would hold onto the reins of our heart and not allow it to venture around so freely. If we were really until now not able to do this in each part of our prayer, which will not be at all easy in the beginning, then at least we try to perform one *dhikr* in our prayer today with presence of our heart and absolute attention.

We do not really notice the level of loss we are incurring upon ourselves due to how inattentive our prayers are. However, one day we will surely realise and we will indeed regret it, and it will be that day of regret that the Quran speaks of:

﴿وَأَنذِرْهُمْ يَوْمَ الْحَسْرَةِ﴾

Warn them of the Day of Regret.[56]

Yes, the punishment of regret is worse than the punishment of Hellfire.

In any case, the path that can further help us in having the presence of the heart in prayer is to pay attention to the spiritual benefits of prayer prior to prayer by a few minutes, with complete attention,

56. Quran, 19:39.

and to think about the consequences and harms of prayer that lack attention.

b) Viewing your Prayer as the Last Prayer

Another method that could further assist us in having presence of the heart in our prayer, which has been mentioned in narrations is thinking about the possibility of this prayer being our last prayer we perform. The noble Prophet (ṣ) thus advised his companions:

صَلِّ صَلاَةَ مُوَدِّعٍ فَإِنَّ فِيهَا ٱلْوُصْلَةَ وَٱلْقُرْبَى

Pray a prayer of one who is bidding farewell because this kind of prayer will connect and bring one near [to Almighty God].[57]

This means that when you want to pray, pray as if it is the very last prayer in your life, and make this prayer your farewell prayer.

How are we really going to know if we will live after this prayer, enough for us to be alive for the next prayer? When we commence our prayer, we cannot have any certainty that we will be able to finish that very prayer itself, so how can we assume that we will be able to pray any other future prayers. If we thought that we only had one opportunity in our life to pray just one prayer, and it will end with "*assalām ʿalaykum wa raḥmatullah wa barakātuhu,*" and then the Angel of death ʿIzrāʾīl will take our souls, we would certainly perform it with much focus and humility before the Almighty.

In every prayer we pray there is such a possibility that it really would be the last prayer we could be performing. Therefore, in every prayer we should turn our complete attention to Almighty God and make

---

57. *Biḥār al-Anwār*, v. 75, p. 200.

the prayer one of repentance, seeking forgiveness and beseeching the Almighty. If we were to just sit down for a few minutes prior to any prayer, and rehearse in our mind that this might be the last prayer we pray in this material world, then this motive will bring about more focus in the prayer.

For example, if you want to travel and it will be a long trip, full of dangers, what will you do? How will you bid farewell to your family members, kin, and friends? During the eight-year imposed Iraq-Iran war, we frequently saw such scenarios, where those joining the battlefront bidding farewell to their family were completely different to how others would bid farewell when travelling somewhere. The mothers and fathers would hug their sons in a very different way, and the farewell of the *mujāhidīn* in the nights before any battle would be very different and unusual. This was all due to the very low likelihood of returning and meeting again.

If someone was to have this kind of a feeling in their prayer, the state and atmosphere of their prayer would be drastically different. If one was to gain such a feeling, that it will be the last time they speak with God, and the last time they prostrate in front of God, then without doubt they will be praying very differently. The farewell prayer will be solemn and heavenly, with weeping eyes, similar to the farewell of the *mujāhidīn* the night before battle. If this was to occur, one will anticipate gaining maximum benefit from this kind of a prayer.

This is the second method to be able to increase one's attention and presence in prayer.

c) Prayer is a Meeting with the Greatest of Great

Another method that can assist you to further concentrate in prayer is to think about who you are turning to, and how majestic they are. The more one thinks about this the more their reverence, veneration and attention will be in their prayer. The person praying must think about who it is they are addressing in their prayer. It is He who knows one's inner-side and is aware of even the smallest thought in his mind and heart. If we were to pay attention to this reality, when we say "*Allahu-akbar*" and commence with reciting al-Fātiḥa, we would not be distracted with thoughts about what we are studying, or reading, or business transactions. Rather, we would be ashamed to address our Creator with our heart being somewhere else because we know that God knows every thought that crosses our mind and He is aware of everything. Of course, reaching such a stage needs practice and repetition.

We must believe that God is present, constantly oversees, is everywhere and nothing is hidden from Him in our movements and our inactivity. In order to acquire this belief in ourselves, we can sit in a room that has a curtain, with nobody else in the room, and then imagine that there is somebody behind the curtain, watching us and what we do. We cannot see who is behind the curtain, but they completely see us and are watching us.

In this scenario, will our actions and our movements be the same between this situation and the other one where we did not imagine anyone behind the curtain? Obviously, it would not be the same. Certainty also has an important role because if you assumed it was probable that someone was monitoring from behind the curtain, you would not behave the same way, even if that person was a young child who is just able to distinguish between good and bad. You would avoid many bad things, or may even avoid doing what is permissible.

We need to practise this kind of state in our prayer. When praying, if we were to feel God's presence at the lowest level – the way we feel in the presence of a normal person – our prayer will be drastically different to how it is now, but then how would it be if we felt the presence of God in His state of divinity? We must at least give God's presence this level of significance that we give to that of a normal person who could be watching us from behind a curtain. If we believe in God's presence to this extent, the presence of our heart will clearly increase. If we were to think about these issues just for a few minutes prior to commencing our prayer, that we are going to meet He who hears our sounds, sees us, and knows what we are feeling in our hearts and minds, we would be in a different state during our prayers.

When Abu Dharr asked the holy Prophet (ṣ) what benevolence was, he said:

اَلْإِحْسَانُ أَنْ تَعْبُدَ اَللّٰهَ كَأَنَّكَ تَرَاهُ، فَإِنْ لَمْ تَكُنْ تَرَاهُ
فَإِنَّهُ يَرَاكَ

Benevolence is that you worship God as if you see Him, and
if you do not see Him, indeed He sees you.[58]

During prayer we must create a live conversation, and not that we are just speaking to someone absent. We must, with our whole existence, perceive God's presence and feel that God is present. In regard to how Imām Jaʿfar al-Ṣādiq (s) was, it is mentioned that one day he was performing a recommended prayer, and while reciting Sūrat al-Ḥamd and another Sūra, he was repeating one of the verses until he fainted. When he was asked, "O son of the Messenger of God, what is this state that we have seen in you?" He replied:

58. *Biḥār al-Anwār*, v. 67, p. 196.

مَـا زِلْـتُ أُكَـرِّرُ آيَـاتِ اَلْقُـرْآنِ حَتَّى بَلَغْـتُ إِلَى حَـالٍ كَأَنَّنِي
سَـمِعْتُ مُشَـافَهَةً مِمَّـنْ أَنْزَلَهَـا

I kept on reciting verses from the Quran until I reached a state where it was as if I could hear the words verbally from He who revealed it.[59]

Yes, they are Infallible Imāms, but experience has proven that reaching such levels or even close to them is something possible to obtain by all the students and real disciples taught by them. They are the great individuals who achieved such states through practice and pursuing the path and teachings of the Imāms, and there are many of them.

Reaching any spiritual level requires practice, exercise and preparing the preliminaries, especially if the levels are considered to be the highest of levels of spiritual perfection. In this regard, one of the preliminary things to do just before praying is to devote a few minutes to think about this, instead of coming straight from our work and saying "Allah-akbar" and commencing our prayer. To hold onto the reins of our hearts, we first need to exercise and concentrate. Prayer means a direct interaction and close conversation with Almighty God. We must have certainty that God hears us and is paying attention to us, and even higher than that, He is aware of what is in our hearts and our inner-thoughts. If during prayer our hearts were somewhere else, we would be like someone turning their back onto the person they are talking to.

If you wanted to speak to a close friend, especially if you treat them with high manners and respect, would you turn your back to them when you are talking to them? It would be considered

59. *Biḥār al-Anwār*, v. 81, p. 247.

extremely offensive and very rude. In our prayer as well, if we were in a conversation with God and our hearts were somewhere else, it would be like turning our backs to God and wanting to talk to Him. Similarly, if we were to turn to ourselves and think about it, we would also realise that it is very impolite and audacious.

It is for this reason that some narrations say should one not be scared to turn their face away in prayer that God will turn (metamorphosis) them into a donkey?[60] This means that the person that does not turn to God during prayer deserves such a punishment, which is to change and undergo metamorphosis (*maskh*) from a human to a donkey. In other words, one who does not observe the etiquette of conversing with God and turns their back away while talking, they are in fact expressing an animalistic trait because an animal does not perceive the etiquette of communicating with someone. When an animal is spoken to, they busily carry on with what they are doing.

Obtaining the State of Humility in Prayer

Another element to utilise from the spirit of prayer is gaining a state of serenity and humility (*khushūʿ*) in prayer. The Holy Quran stresses on humility in prayer, as the Almighty has said:

﴿قَد أَفلَحَ المُؤمِنونَ ۞ الَّذينَ هُم في صَلاتِهِم خاشِعونَ﴾

Certainly, the faithful have attained salvation —those who are humble in their prayers.[61]

In another place, the Almighty says:

60. See: *Biḥār al-Anwār*, v. 81, p. 211, ḥ. 3.

61. Quran, 23:1–2.

﴿وَاسْتَعِينُوا بِالصَّبْرِ وَالصَّلَاةِ وَإِنَّهَا لَكَبِيرَةٌ إِلَّا عَلَى الْخَاشِعِينَ﴾

And seek help through patience and prayer, and indeed, it is difficult except for the humbly submissive [to Allah].[62]

a) The Meaning of Humility

It is difficult to find an English equivalent for the term Arabic *khushūʿ* that correctly explains its meaning, but looking into how the Quran uses this term could assist us in better clarifying its meaning.

One instance where the Quran uses this word is in relation to sound, explaining the qualities and state of Judgment Day. The Almighty says:

﴿وَخَشَعَتِ الْأَصْوَاتُ لِلرَّحْمَٰنِ فَلَا تَسْمَعُ إِلَّا هَمْسًا﴾

The voices will be muted before the All-beneficent, and you will hear nothing but a murmur.[63]

On Judgement Day, God's awe and greatness will appear, and hence only whispers and low voices will be heard. On that day, each and every person will say something but because Almighty God's presence will dominate everything, nobody will be able to talk loudly due to the intensity of God's great existence. As the verse says: *and you will hear nothing but a murmur.*[64] Nobody will be able to talk in a loud voice, and this is what the Quranic verse refers to in 'humility of voices' (one's volume of voice is lower than normal and unable to speak with confidence).

62. Quran, 2:45.
63. Quran, 20:108.
64. Quran, 20:108.

Another case where the Holy Quran uses the expression of *khushūʿ* is *khushūʿ* of faces, as the Almighty says:

﴿وُجوهٌ يَومَئِذٍ خاشِعَةٌ﴾

Some faces on that day will be humbled.[65]

It apparently seems that this verse is referring to the faces of the felonious disbelievers. On Judgement Day, the faces of the disbelievers and sinners will be humiliated.[66]

In order to perceive the concept of *khushūʿ* and understand its state, it is firstly necessary to realise that *khushūʿ* is not a state of pretending or acting. It is possible for someone to do something that externally shows a state of *khushūʿ* in their face and body, but this *khushūʿ* is not real, because real *khushūʿ* stems from the heart. Before anything, it is the heart that must have *khushūʿ*, and then that *khushūʿ* flows to other parts of the outer body and movement. The Quran says:

﴿أَلَم يَأنِ لِلَّذينَ آمَنوا أَن تَخشَعَ قُلوبُهُم لِذِكرِ اللَّهِ وَما نَزَلَ مِنَ الحَقِّ﴾

Is it not time yet for those who have faith that their hearts should be humbled for Allah's remembrance and to the truth which has come down [*to them*].[67]

This is a form of reproaching, saying is it not time for the believers to have *khushūʿ* when remembering God

65. Quran, 88:2.
66. There are other verses in the Holy Quran that use this word, but this is outside of our current discussion. What we wanted to briefly explain is the concept of *khushūʿ* by mentioning some of the instances of this term in the Quran.
67. Quran, 57:16.

According to the Holy Quran, one of the special characteristics of this Noble Book is that people who have pure and good nature when they hear the Quran their skin quivers. The Almighty says:

﴿اللَّهُ نَزَّلَ أَحْسَنَ الْحَدِيثِ كِتَابًا مُتَشَابِهًا مَثَانِيَ تَقْشَعِرُّ مِنْهُ جُلُودُ الَّذِينَ يَخْشَوْنَ رَبَّهُمْ﴾

Allah has sent down the best of discourses, a scripture [composed] of similar motifs, whereat quiver the skins of those who fear their Lord.[68]

Of course, this state is an instantaneous state that does not continue, so it occurs for an instance and then finishes. As for how this state appears, it is something that psychologists need to explain. It is similar to an involuntary reaction that we do towards natural movements. If there is a very loud sound, we would naturally shake from where we are and move. This is an involuntary state, regarded as a natural reaction. There are some perceptions similar to this, where the body involuntarily trembles under certain circumstances and as a result of specific perceptions. It is obvious that someone who has not experienced such a state will not be able to perceive its reality, but the Quran says that there are people who have reached such a state as a result of listening to the Quran.

To further clarify this concept, let's assume that someone enters a house and thinks that there is nobody home. He takes his formal attire off and goes about his ways very comfortably and without any concern, eating, drinking, and relaxing. While in this state, he suddenly hears a sound inside the house, and of course he will naturally be scared once hearing it. He will say to himself that nobody was home, so where did this sound come from, because he was absolutely sure he was

68. Quran, 39:23.

all alone. When the door suddenly opens and somebody enters, he will be shocked and scared. This kind of state cannot be described if someone has not experienced it himself. It is a normal state and natural reaction to a surrounding movement. If that person who came in was a member of the household, this person's state will quickly return to its normal condition and all fear will go away.

The Quran says that this will be the natural result for those who have still preserved their natural primordial disposition and listen to verses of the Quran. With hearing the Quran, they experience a kind of shock that sends tremors through their skin: *whereat quiver the skins of those who fear their Lord.*[69] This is because they believe and know Almighty God. After those first instances when they see that the Almighty whom they recognise is speaking to them, they quickly return to their natural state and feel tranquillity and safety:

﴿ثُمَّ تَلِينُ جُلُودُهُم وَقُلوبُهُم إِلَىٰ ذِكرِ اللَّهِ﴾

Then their skins and hearts soften to Allah's remembrance.[70]

Not only do they not get disturbed, but they enjoy God and they become engulfed with a special kind of tranquillity, spreading to their spirit and heart. They initially thought it was foreign and unknown, but they then quickly realise it is the Merciful Beloved giving them inner-peace and tranquillity. Of course, on the opposite side there are people who when God is mentioned in front of them, they feel His presence and they are annoyed and disturbed, because they are foreign to God. Regarding such people, the Almighty says:

69. Quran, 39:23.
70. Quran, 39:23.

﴿وَإِذَا ذُكِرَ اللَّهُ وَحْدَهُ اشْمَأَزَّتْ قُلُوبُ الَّذِينَ لَا يُؤْمِنُونَ بِالْآخِرَةِ﴾

When Allah is mentioned alone, [thereat] shrink away the hearts of those who do not believe in the Hereafter.[71]

However, those who know God and their souls have the potential of being amicable with Him, after the initial feeling, they realise they are in the presence of God, and based on the level of their recognition (*maʿrifa*) and according to the level of their perception of the greatness of their Lord they will experience a level of *khushūʿ* and veneration.

The following example and comparison will be given to further clarify what is meant here. Imagine there is a soldier who falls asleep for an instance while on duty, thinking nobody else is around. Suddenly he opens his eyes, seeing his commanding officer standing above him. How would you think this soldier would feel in such a situation?

Without doubt, the soldier would be very nervous and ashamed, along with being scared as well. The awe and greatness of the commander would make the soldier stumble and get disoriented. He would also be embarrassed that he had fallen asleep on duty. The higher the rank the commander is, the more unsteady and fearful the soldier will be, mixed with more and more shame. There is a direct connection between perceiving the greatness of the person and the intensity of the reaction. Believers experience this kind of feeling towards the greatness of God. The level of their humility (*khuḍūʿ*) connects with the level of their perception and recognition of God's greatness.

---

71. Quran, 39:45.

It is this kind of reaction that we have explained in this example that could somehow occur to any person in their lives, and is the state most comparable and closest to the state of *khushūʿ*.

There is a correlation between *khushūʿ* and the state of bewilderment, and we are compelled to give yet another example to bring closer the meaning and explain it. If there was a high-profile distinguished person who, for example, had a PhD degree or a university lecturer, and after a period that people have known him in such a position it is suddenly revealed that his claim was false. Not only did he not have a doctorate degree, but he was illiterate. In this situation, one would automatically have a strong reaction, shocked, with the colour of their face changing, breaking down, and so on.

Of course, there is a difference between *khushūʿ* for God and *khushūʿ* for people. *Khuḍūʿ* and *khushūʿ* towards people is something hurtful that brings about pain and is severe to handle. However, if this state occurs towards Almighty God, it will be accompanied with pleasure. Some eminent scholars have said that the pleasure one experiences with God that results in shedding of tears is the highest level of pleasure in this world, so much that they would wish they had nothing other than this state, and for it to continue forever.

Yes, there are those who are ready to replace all the pleasures of the world with one instance of this state. All of this is because *khushūʿ* is fundamentally something instinctive, and human instinct necessitates that a human being does not see themselves as independent or as an entity in front of God. The believer sees all existence, including himself, connecting to God.

No matter what characteristics a person has in knowledge, power, beauty and perfection, they are all reflections of the absolute Perfection, Beauty, Knowledge and Power of the Almighty. If we were to perceive this reality and understand it through presential-knowledge (*ʿilm ḥuḍūrī*), we would certainly have *khushūʿ* and the more *khushūʿ* we have the higher our level becomes.

b) Humility is Negating the "I"

How can the heart be broken (*inkisār al-qalb*), and what does this mean? The breaking of the heart occurs when one is inflicted with a tribulation and falls in desperate and serious need. When someone is incapable of doing anything and loses hope in receiving help from all those around him, that is when the heart becomes broken. This state, however, is not *khushūʿ*, because *khushūʿ* is something higher and loftier than this, as *khushūʿ* occurs when the fort of the "I" (*al-anāniyyah*) and the ego (*al-maniyyah*) are destroyed.

We all see ourselves as a personality and an independent identity, or in other words, the I and the ego. According to Islamic morals and Islamic teachings, our biggest problem and deficiency comes from this very issue. This problem reaches its peak when we feel the "I-ness" against the Almighty. This kind of state in a human is considered as audacious, even if it is towards other people, but such a feeling does not result in a horrendous plight and losing value of their actions. As for I-ness towards God, this basically means "O Lord, You are You, and I am I!". This state of being forms a basis for deviation and all types of human corruption. If such a feeling was to continue and reach its peak, its possessor will get to a stage where he will proclaim:

﴿أَنَا رَبُّكُمُ الأَعلَىٰ﴾

'I am your exalted lord!' [72]

72. Quran, 79:24.

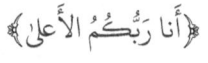

When Pharaoh proclaimed this sentence, he was revealing his highest egoism and "I-ness".

As for prayer, it is showing the state of devotion and submission to God and His law. Prayer is submission to the Will of God and overlooking one's own will.

Everyone must put in a lot of effort—especially the young—to ensure that their course is guided by Divine intent, and they must train themselves from the start to base all their acts and behaviour on this principle. Furthermore, we should not just be giving instructions, with others obeying them and serving them, but to also strive harder to serve people as well. If a youth from an early age was to repeat and practice these two things, the Pharaonic spirit and I-ness will become weaker instead of stronger. If from the beginning we were to know what our duties are in everything and what God wants from us, we would not fall into the trap of I-ness or drown in the whirlpool of:

﴿مَنِ اتَّخَذَ إِلَٰهَهُ هَوَاهُ﴾

He who has taken his desire to be his god?[73]

c) Outer *Khushūʿ* and Inner *Khushūʿ*

In any case, before subjecting oneself to being disciplined by Prophets and divine instructors, humans suffer a level of I-ness and egotism, and therefore one must try to think about correcting one's own self and fixing it in the first instance. If we do not monitor and fix ourselves, our dam of I-ness will fortify itself and become stronger, so much so that it cannot be easily demolished and will be very difficult to fall apart.

73. Quran, 25:43.

﴿وَلَا يَكُونُوا كَالَّذِينَ أُوتُوا الْكِتَابَ مِنْ قَبْلُ فَطَالَ عَلَيْهِمُ الْأَمَدُ فَقَسَتْ قُلُوبُهُمْ﴾

And to be not like those who were given the Book before? but long ages passed over them and so their hearts were hardened.[74]

Some reach such a stage where their hearts, as the Quran expresses, becomes so hard, stronger than a rock. Almighty God described the hardness of the hearts of Bani Israel, saying:

﴿ثُمَّ قَسَتْ قُلُوبُكُمْ مِنْ بَعْدِ ذَٰلِكَ فَهِيَ كَالْحِجَارَةِ أَوْ أَشَدُّ قَسْوَةً وَإِنَّ مِنَ الْحِجَارَةِ لَمَا يَتَفَجَّرُ مِنْهُ الْأَنْهَارُ وَإِنَّ مِنْهَا لَمَا يَشَّقَّقُ فَيَخْرُجُ مِنْهُ الْمَاءُ وَإِنَّ مِنْهَا لَمَا يَهْبِطُ مِنْ خَشْيَةِ اللَّهِ﴾

Then your hearts hardened after that; so they are like stones, or even harder. For indeed there are some stones from which streams gush forth, and indeed there are some of them that split, and water issues from them, and indeed there are some of them that fall for the fear of Allah.[75]

Some people's hearts have become so hard that their eyes do not even shed one tear. Their hearts have become harder than a rock, but opposite to them are those whose hearts quickly break like a wall that can collapse at any moment. This is one of the stages and levels of breaking of the heart, where the wall of the human heart is fragile and weak.

Sometimes, the broken heart is so intense that the wall of the heart has a deep crack, and at times it could be like a house that collapses

74. Quran, 57:16.
75. Quran, 2:74.

with its walls and roof all at once. In this case, the wall of the human ego will collapse all at once, not leaving any trace, as if there was no house or no wall. Complete *khushūʿ* is this latter case, with crumbling the walls of the heart, turning them into ashes and being taken away by strong winds.

If someone were to acquire such a state – breaking and crumbling of their heart – whether they like it or not, it will involuntarily have affects appearing on their face and outer appearance. For example, their voice will unwillingly be hesitant and humble, and if someone was to pray in such a state, they will be an example of what the following holy verse refers to:

﴿قَد أَفلَحَ المُؤمِنونَ ۝ الَّذينَ هُم في صَلاتِهِم خاشِعونَ﴾

Certainly, the faithful have attained salvation —those who are humble in their prayers.[76]

Khushūʿ is not pretending, or altering of voice tone during prayer, or sloping one's head or neck. All these are examples of pretending, and not real *khushūʿ*. If in reality a heart was broken, then that wall of "I" would tremble, and the house of idols would collapse. The effects of this will also clearly and involuntarily be apparent in one's face, appearance and behaviour.

A question might arise here, and that is whether it is correct for someone to reach such a state? Those who have not lived the experience of connecting with God and consider this state a sign of a weak personality, saying if someone's heart is broken and if one shakes and weeps, with a feeble voice, then this rather shows weakness in their personality and mental state.

---

76. Quran, 23:1–2.

Opposite to this are those who believe in God, know God and perceive His greatness, and they believe that the absence of such a state signifies a deficiency and a problem. As for us, we believe that this is fundamentally necessitated by human nature. When a human being considers that they are essentially nothing, and everything comes from God, then what false state is it that stands against God? What is the reason that would make someone build that cement wall of "I" in front of their Lord? The problem is for one to perceive their own self separate and opposite to God.

d) The Difference Between *al-Khushūʿ*, *al-Khawf* and *al-Khashyah*

As previously mentioned, *khushūʿ* is experiencing a special feeling of reverence, humility and breaking of the self, accompanied by a state of awe (*al-khashya*) and fear (*al-khawf*). Therefore, to further explain the concept of *khushūʿ*, we must discuss the concept of *khashya* and *khawf*, and the difference between them and their connection.

In the Holy Quran, we read the following verse:

﴿لَو أَنزَلنا هٰذَا القُرآنَ عَلىٰ جَبَلٍ لَرَأَيتَهُ خاشِعًا مُتَصَدِّعًا
مِن خَشيَةِ اللَّهِ﴾

Had We sent down this Quran upon a mountain, you would have surely seen it humbled [and] go to pieces with the fear of Allah.[77]

According to this verse, if the Quran was to have descended onto a mountain, the mountain would have *khushūʿ* and tremor, so much that it would disintegrate. In this verse, the Almighty used both concepts of *khushūʿ* and *khashya* together.

77. Quran, 59:21.

The meaning of *khashya* might usually not be that correctly clear for us. It is a term that is commonly correlated with the word *khawf* (fear) or related to the term solemnity (*hayba*). Many of us think that these three words (*al-khushūʿ*, *al-khawf*, *al-khashya*) are synonymous and give the same meaning, but that is not the case. The word *hayba* is also usually wrongly used where one would say: "so and so person has this *hayba*", or "I felt such and such a state from his *hayba*." We attribute *hayba* to a person, but in fact *hayba* is the state in which a person experiences when perceiving the greatness of the other person.

When we face someone who has astonishing greatness, we feel insignificant and nondescript in their presence, feeling a level of brokenness and yielding. In such a state, we would say: "My tongue was twisted by the awe of so and so, and I was not able to utter one word." As mentioned, *hayba* is in fact a characteristic and state we experience because of knowing how great that person is.

The state of *hayba* could be connected with recognition and other elements as well. After knowing the greatness of a person and recognising who they are, this could make one realise what great person they impudently opposed. This is why, in addition to *khashya* that occurs as a result of knowing the greatness of that person, the state of *khushūʿ* also occurs. At times, other than these two states, one feels that they deserve punishment because of their insolence and sin that they had committed towards that great individual. This great individual has also prepared various punishments for disobeyers, and this is what brings about the state of fear, along with the state of veneration and humility.

It is not always necessary for the two states of *khashya* and *khushūʿ* to occur with fear, and they could also not occur due to having the state of fear from divine punishment, or it could occur solely due to being affected by the realisation of God's greatness. For example, disobedience and sinning are not involved with the mountain to say that the mountain had *khashya* and *khushūʿ* out of fear of God's punishment. Rather, the disintegrating of the mountain occurred as a result of perceiving God's greatness.

Therefore, the state of *khashya*, bewilderment and fear due to being in the presence of Almighty God is more general than when they occur as a result of feeling sinful or because of fear of punishment or purely because of perceiving God's greatness. One of these states that one would experience is the paling of their facial complexion, their body shivering when they stand in front of a great personality and overwhelmed with what seems to be fear, but this state is not necessarily due to punishment, as it could be an effect of how great that personality is. It is narrated that when Imām Ḥasan al-Mujtabā (ʿa) would perform his ablution, his body would shake and his colour would turn yellow.[78] It is also narrated that when Lady Fāṭima al-Zahrāʾ (ʿa) would stand in her prayer niche for worship, her whole body would tremble, and while in this state, Almighty God would say to His angels:

يَـا مَلاَئِكَتِي أُنْظُـرُوا إِلَى أَمَتِي فَاطِمَـةَ سَـيِّدَةِ إِمَـائِي قَائِمَـةً بَيْنَ
يَـدِيَّ تَرْتَعِـدُ فَرَائِصُهَـا مِـنْ خِيـفَتِي وَ قَـدْ أَقْبَلَـتْ بِقَلْبِهَـا عَلَى
عِبَـادَتِي أُشْـهِدُكُمْ أَنِّي قَـدْ آمَنْـتُ شِـيعَتَهَا مِـنَ اَلنَّار

O My angels, look at my servant Fāṭimah al-Zahrāʾ, the Lady of My servants, standing in prayer before me, her limbs shaking out of fear of Me, coming to Me with her whole heart in worshipping Me.

78. Ibn Shahrāshūb, *Manāqib Āl Abī Ṭālib*, ed. group of scholars from Najaf Seminary v. 4, p. 14.

In summary, with this explanation it becomes clear that *khushūʿ* comes about due to various reasons. It could occur purely as a result of perceiving the status of God's greatness, or due to being ashamed in sinning and disobeying Almighty God, or because of fear of divine punishment.

The Relation Between Love and Humility

When a person has a loved one whom they are unable to reach and cannot see, they will live in an ongoing state of restlessness and yearning. This state could reach its peak when the person knows their beloved sees them and knows of their state and condition, whereas they cannot see their beloved or do not have any information about them. When Imām Ḥusain (ʿa) turned to the Almighty in his supplication of ʿArafa, saying:

عَمِيَتْ عَيْنٌ لا تَراكَ عَلَيْها رَقيباً

Blind are the eyes that cannot see You as an Overseer upon them

If one was to truly delve into this matter, they must firstly deepen their inner-knowledge of Almighty God and become more acquainted with Him. The more you know God and further perceive His Majesty, the greater your love will be for Him and ultimately this love will reside and encompass your heart. When love of God occupies the heart, the flame of yearning to meet Him will ignite and one will lose patience in anticipation of meeting his Beloved. As a result, when you stand to pray, your heart will be at awe due to longing for this connection and will go through this state of humility. The question now is what do we do to surpass these levels and reach such spiritual states?

The Best Way to Create Love of God in the Heart

The best way to create love of Almighty God in the heart is how He Himself has taught us. In a ḥadīth qudsī, Almighty God addressed Prophet Moses (s), saying:

حَبِّبْنِي إِلَى خَلْقِي وَحَبِّبْ خَلْقِي إِلَيَّ. قَالَ: يَا رَبِّ كَيْفَ أَفْعَلُ؟ قَالَ: ذَكِّرْهُمْ آلاَئِي وَنَعْمَائِي

Love Me and make My creation love Me. Prophet Moses asked: O Lord, how can I do that? The Almighty replied: Remind them of My favours and My bounties.[79]

The human being's innate nature is such that it loves one who does good to them. Almighty God stresses on this point as well when He says to Prophet Moses remind people of the bounties I have blessed them with, and all the good and grace I have descended upon them. If people were to take notice of this, their instinct would automatically direct them to loving God, and the more people notice these blessings and favours bestowed upon them, the more they will love the Almighty.

The method this narration gives is one of the best ways of obtaining love of God, and it is an easy and accessible way that can be recommended for anyone to pursue. Of course, the paths taken by God's saints and the virtuous who have reached high levels of righteousness, and as a result of perceiving complete love, are more meticulous, deeper and subtler than the state of this mentioned path. Nonetheless, this is a way open in front of us average people. If we tried to truly comprehend God's blessings and perceive them, along

---

79. *Biḥār al-Anwār*, v. 2, p. 4, h. 6.

with thoroughly looking into its effects in our life, we will naturally love God, and this love will reach our heart so much that it will consume it.

There are no boundaries or limits to enumerate God's bounties and blessings towards us. In reality, we are oblivious to the oceans of His favours, and incapable of counting them, as much as we try to comprehend. Among these bounties that we can think about are those that we were unable to attain, like situations that have somehow occurred in our lives. There are many instances or situations where we were in need, and our affairs became so complicated, with all doors closing in our faces, losing hope, and being in such a dire state when God's grace encompassed us and unexpectedly solved our problems. In these cases, or situations, we would enter a special state and feel shy and broken in front of God. We would uncontrollably shed tears of longing, and this yearning comes from feeling how God's grace included this nondescript servant who is not worth anything.[80]

---

80. This state of a broken heart does not just occur when facing calamities or noticing divine punishment. At times, it could come from intense yearning for the Almighty, or from feeling ashamed. The humility towards God does not necessarily come from the realisation God's power, wrath and punishment as well. The important thing is that the heart is soft and inclined to shedding tears, where such a state could come about as a result of yearning and infatuation. An example for this is what can be seen in the following Quranic verse, describing some of the Christians:
﴿لَتَجِدَنَّ أَشَدَّ النَّاسِ عَدَاوَةً لِلَّذِينَ آمَنُوا الْيَهُودَ وَالَّذِينَ أَشْرَكُوا ۖ وَلَتَجِدَنَّ أَقْرَبَهُمْ مَوَدَّةً لِلَّذِينَ آمَنُوا الَّذِينَ قَالُوا إِنَّا نَصَارَىٰ ۚ ذَٰلِكَ بِأَنَّ مِنْهُمْ قِسِّيسِينَ وَرُهْبَانًا وَأَنَّهُمْ لَا يَسْتَكْبِرُونَ ۝ وَإِذَا سَمِعُوا مَا أُنْزِلَ إِلَى الرَّسُولِ تَرَىٰ أَعْيُنَهُمْ تَفِيضُ مِنَ الدَّمْعِ مِمَّا عَرَفُوا مِنَ الْحَقِّ﴾
Surely You will find the most hostile of all people towards the faithful to be the Jews and the polytheists, and surely you will find the nearest of them in affection to the faithful to be those who say 'We are Christians.' That is because there are priests and monks among them, and because they are not arrogant. When they hear what has been revealed to the Apostle, you see their eyes fill with tears because of the truth that they recognize. [Quran, 5:82–83]
There were a group of Christians and monastics who were far away

If we were to remember that state in which Almighty God granted us that unexpected blessing instantaneously, given to us who are lowly, our memory would revitalise us and we would bring back that state of yearning and softness of the heart that was given to us during that time. If we were to ponder on that state and what it brings in specific blessings, placing this right in front of us and remembering it, then allowing it to flow to our other blessings, this will gradually increase our yearning, infatuation, and love of Almighty God. If this was to repeat, it could gradually turn into a fixed disposition (*malaka*), and in all states of yearning of blessings that God has endowed upon us, we feel in our hearts the love and yearning for Him.

God's blessings are not just the blessings that we usually notice. The whole world in its entirety are blessings for humankind. Imām Ḥusain (ʿa) mentions the detailed and subtle blessings and bounties of the Almighty, when counting and noticing them. Indeed, we must learn from Imām Ḥusain (ʿa) and enumerate these divine bounties in the same way. When he stood on the Day of ʿArafa under the sun in the scorching heat, shedding tears like rain from his blessed eyes, and in such a state he mentioned these bounties, starting with the light of vision, details of the body, teeth, heart, kidney, and other limbs, saying:

فَأَيُّ أَنْعُمِكَ يَا إِلَهِي أُحْصِي عَدَداً أَوْ ذِكْراً أَمْ أَيُّ عَطَائِكَ
أَقُومُ بِهَا شُكْراً وَهِيَ يَا رَبِّ أَكْثَرُ مِنْ أَنْ يُحْصِيَهَا ٱلْعَادُّونَ

from arrogance, and they were in such a state that if they witnessed or heard some of the signs in the Quran and the Torah, because of how intense their yearning for recognising God was, their eyes would involuntarily shed tears. When they realised that this was the Prophet that Jesus had foretold in the Gospels, they felt such admiration, yearning and thankfulness that tears flowed from their eyes.

أَوْ يَبْلُغَ عِلْماً بِهَا ٱلْحَافِظُونَ...وَأَنَا أُشْهِدُكَ يَا إِلَهِي بِحَقِيقَةِ
إِيمَانِي... وَعَلاَئِقِ مَجَارِي نُورِ بَصَرِي وَ أَسَارِيرِ صَفْحَةِ
جَبِينِي وَخُرْقِ مَسَارِبِ نَفْسِي وَخَذَارِيفِ مَارِنِ عِرْنِينِي
وَمَسَارِبِ صِمَاخِ سَمْعِي وَمَا ضُمَّتْ وَأُطْبِقَتْ عَلَيْهِ
شَفَتَايَ وَحَرَكَاتُ لَفْظِ لِسَانِي وَمَغْرَزِ حَنَكِ فَمِي وَفَكِّي وَ
مَنَابِتِ أَضْرَاسِي وَبُلُوغِ حَبَائِلِ بَارِعِ عُنُقِي... وَمَا حَوَتْهُ
شَرَاسِيفُ أَضْلاَعِي وَحِقَاقِ مَفَاصِلِي وَأَطْرَافِ أَنَامِلِي
وَقَبْضِ عَوَامِلِي وَدَمِي وَشَعْرِي وَبَشَرِي وَعَصَبِي وَقَصَبِي
وَعِظَامِي وَمُخِّي وَعُرُوقِي وَجَمِيعِ جَوَارِحِي

Which of Your favours, O my God, can I count in numbers and examples? Or which of Your gifts can I thank properly? O my Lord, they are too numerous to be counted by counters or to be realised by memorisers.... And I bear witness, O my God, with my true belief... and the ties of the canals of the light of my sight, and the lines of my forehead and the hallows of the courses of my breath, and the (nasal) cavities of my nose, and the courses of the meatus of my hearing, and whatever my two lips hide and cover up, and the motions of the vocalization of my tongue, and the socket of the palate of my mouth and jaw, and the matrices of my dents, and the tasting of my food and my drink, and the carrier of my skill, and the tube of the tissues of my neck... and that which is included by the cartilages of my ribs, and the cavities of my joints, and the interactions of my organisms, and the extremes of my fingertips, and my flesh, and my blood, and my hair, and my skin, and my nerve, and my sinews, and my bones, and my brain, and my veins, and all of my organs.[81]

81. *Biḥār al-Anwār*, v. 91, Section 32, h. 21, p. 151.

How graceful indeed is Almighty God towards us. If He had not granted us each of these blessings, how many deficiencies, illnesses and difficulties would we have. Furthermore, something that is greater than that are the spiritual divine blessings that we seldomly pay attention to or care about.

The Ahlul Bayt (ʿa) always focused on the spiritual divine blessings in their supplications and whispered prayers (*munājāt*).[82] Imām ʿAlī al-Sajjād (ʿa) says in his *Munājāt al-Dhākirīn* (*The Whispered Prayers of the Rememberers*)[83]:

وَمِنْ أَعْظَمِ النِّعَمِ عَلَيْنا جَرَيانُ ذِكْرِكَ عَلى أَلْسِنَتِنا،
وَإِذْنُكَ لَنا بِدُعآئِكَ

And among Your greatest favours upon us is the running of Your remembrance across our tongues and Your permission to us to supplicate to You.[84]

We might not have even thought about this, in being allowed to address Almighty God and speak with Him. We would see that we are not at His level if we were to contrast our insignificance and frailty with His majesty and divine power, and that we should not be permitted to stand in His mighty presence and ask to talk with Him.

---

82. The word *Munājāt* has been translated into English in various ways, like confidential talk, intimate whispering, intimate orison, and so on.

83. This is the thirteenth of the fifteen *Munājāts* of Imām ʿAlī al-Sajjād (ʿa)

84. See: ʿAlī Ibn al-Ḥusayn Zayn al-ʿĀbidīn, *Al-Ṣaḥīfah al-Sajjādiyyah al-Kāmilah* (*The Psalms of Islam*), translated & introduced by William Chittick (Qom: Ansarian Publications, 2009) pp. 524–525. Also see: Shaykh Abbas Qummi, *Mafātiḥ al-Jinān: A Treasury of Islamic Piety: Volume One: Supplications and Periodic Observances*, translated by Ali Quli Qarai (2019) *Munājāt,* p. 360.

We could be told in this world what the dwellers of Hellfire will be told in the Hereafter:

﴿اخْسَئُوا فِيهَا وَلَا تُكَلِّمُونِ﴾

Be despised in there! Do not [ever] plead with Me [again]![85]

Who then will be able to speak and open their mouth to talk?

Not every person has the right or entitlement to talk in front of Almighty God. If it was not for Him to allow us to talk, we would not have the worthiness of speaking with Him. Imagine a great gathering attended by distinguished personalities and high-ranking officials, and in this gathering, not everyone is able to talk, unless previously authorised. When being in front of Almighty God whose greatness has no limit, we the poor nondescript creatures who have nothing but what He has bestowed upon us, are not able and should not move our tongues to speak except with His permission. Of course, based on the infinite grace and mercy of Almighty God, He has allowed all His creation to turn to Him and converse with Him, but if that was not the case, nobody could on their own accord grant themselves to have such a right.

It is for this reason that among the greatest of divine favours over creation is allowing us to converse with Him, and we have not only received this privilege, but we have also been invited and commanded to hasten towards Him every day and night, numerous times, in the form of prayer, to converse with Him. Think about how the beloved holds a greater and higher rank and status than that of the lover. That social and ranking distance that separates this Beloved and this lover will not even allow the lover to get close to the realm of the Beloved.

---

85. Quran, 23:108.

Now imagine this Beloved sending a letter to the lover, saying: "I am waiting to see you and meet you." How would the lover feel? With so much excitement and happiness, they might not be able to stay in their own body, and unwillingly shed tears of joy. All this grace and glory from the Beloved will result in the lover's soul breaking away from the body and ascending to the beloved. The state of prayer is similar to this, or even greater. We are the poor and the insignificant, and God is the infinite greatness above any level of imagination, and a great one has sent this nondescript letter, saying hasten to Him so that you can receive the splendour of being in His presence and talking to Him.

Now think about how much wrong we have done to this Beloved and how continuously harsh and audacious we are towards Him without any shame. If one day a group of people were to rush to His gathering and be in His great presence, and I was also among this group who had our heads down, withdrawn in the corner of the gathering. If He does not expel me in that state from the gathering, this itself would be a great favour.

However, the Sublime invites me to His proximity, and to the closest station to Him as well. Not only is He not banishing me but is so kindly and compassionately asking about me. How would I really feel in this situation? Almighty God has bestowed upon us the greatest grace, inviting us to prayer, and revealing how great He is, beyond any form of description. He did not banish us because of our recurring disobedience and sin, but rather He requested us to be present in His divine presence. Instead of us being the ones who implore and beg for our Lord to open a path towards His doorstep, giving us an instance to pray to him, but He is the one who is requesting that we benefit from the bounties of meeting Him.

If we were to pay attention to this point that Almighty God with all His might and splendour has allowed this sinful inconsiderable servant to talk to Him and to turn to Him, then our yearning and excitement to want to meet Him will overwhelm us, such that it cannot be described in words. This yearning and excitement, does not resemble any normal yearning or excitement, and does not happen to everyone. This is *khushūʿ* that comes from yearning and from love.

Comparing the Greatness of Spiritual Bounties with Material Bounties

If someone wants to increase their love of Almighty God, they must start with looking at the bounties and special favours God has bestowed upon them, and work towards thinking about them in their mind. These circumstances occur in every human, when they are in dire need and then God hears their call and takes their hand. This kind of invocation and remembrance must flow to all other bounties, because each of the divine blessings have an important role on their own, similar to blessings that are unexpectedly bestowed upon us. If the least defect occurs in any part of our body, as small as it may be, we will realise how great a blessing it was that we were inattentive to.

The third level, in addition to taking notice of the material blessings, is to take notice of the spiritual blessings that come from Almighty God's auspices. This is because the value of many of the spiritual blessings are much more than material blessings. When we are a guest, one way the host honours us is to put effort and prepare appropriate food for us, but we feel more honoured when the host receives us with a smile and warm welcoming and shows love and extra care to us. One smile, or one caring gaze or a kind word from the host will be of more value for us than their invitation or the food they serve.

This kind of spiritual blessing when compared to food and material blessing will hold greater value. Spiritual blessings of Almighty God are like this. A person of religious understanding (*maʿrifa*) would understand that some divine blessings cannot be compared with absolutely all the material blessings that come from Him. Those who are closer to Him feel the pleasure of these blessings even more. There are blessings that God has prepared only for His close and elite servants, and they are blessings that cannot be described or even imagined:

أَعْدَدْتُ لِعِبَادِيَ ٱلصَّالِحِينَ مَا لاَ عَيْنٌ رَأَتْ وَلاَ أُذُنٌ سَمِعَتْ
وَلاَ خَطَرَ عَلَى قَلْبِ بَشَرٍ

I have prepared for my pious servant what no eye has ever seen, no ear has ever heard and no human heart has ever conceived.[86]

Ways of Producing *Khushūʿ* in Prayer

1. Turning to God's Greatness

For *khushūʿ* to manifest in us during prayer, we must think about something beforehand, and that is to try and perceive how great Almighty God is, and to compare God's greatness with our insignificance, based on our understanding and capacity of comprehension.

Therefore, understanding God's greatness leads to *khushūʿ*, and if we want to achieve *khushūʿ* in our prayer, the most effective of ways

86. *Biḥār al-Anwār*, v. 33, p. 82, h. 397.

is to perceive how great Almighty God is. Our primary question now is how are we able to get this kind of understanding?

To understand God's greatness, we must first see what we conceive in our minds about this. When we say:

﴿الْعَلِيُّ الْعَظِيمُ﴾

The All-exalted, the All-supreme.[87]

What concept do we conceive in our minds about God's greatness (*'aẓama*)? We are limited material creatures, and we rarely succeed in perceiving immaterial concepts. Therefore, we must try to strengthen our understanding and elevate it.

Nonetheless, regarding God's exaltedness and greatness, we need to first start with material concepts. At first, we perceive God's greatness through its physical referents that come from the category of quantity (*maqūlat al-kam*).[88] When we say "this is something great," we mean its size is large, and if its length, width and height are larger, we would say it is greater. Then there are things that exist that do not have a size, and are not physical, but we also refer to them with the concept of greatness and largeness.

For example, we say a person's spirit is great, even though a spirit/soul is not physical and does not have a material essence. When we say this, we do not mean the size of their soul is larger than that of others, but we have no way to express it other than by saying it in this way. We are forced to use these same terms that carry material meanings. The technical term for this is "expansion of the concept," which means the concept that was primarily made for a material

87. Quran, 2:255.

88. This refers to one of the ten Aristotelian categories.

meaning is used for an immaterial meaning. We say this greatness is not restricted to the largeness of a body, but there is spiritual greatness as well. Therefore, when we use this description of greatness for our Lord, we are also using these same terms as well, but the referent of greatness in His case is completely different to physical greatness, or even spiritual greatness.

In any case, we do not have many options because our minds fundamentally cannot perceive the concept of greatness except by comparing it in greatness of sizes, and we are very much like ants in this case. Imām Muḥammad al-Bāqir ('a) says:

ولعلّ النّمل الصّغار تتوهّم أنّ لله تعالى زبانيين، فإنّ ذلك كمالها ويتوهّم أنّ عدمهما نقصان لمن لا يتصّف بهما.

It might be that small ants think that Almighty God has two antennas, assuming that not having antennas would be considered a deficiency for one who is not described as having them.[89]

We are the same. We initially think that Almighty God is like this, as we understand God being the *All-Exalted* (*al-ʿalī*) and the *All-Supreme* (*al-ʿaẓīm*) in material forms, assuming that God's exaltedness is that He is higher than the heavens. This is because we do not primarily conceive any exaltedness other than material exaltedness. We must gradually put pressure on our minds to remove these polluted material concepts and similarities that we use in relation to God. In the first states, our understanding of God being the *All-Exalted* and the *All-Supreme* are connected to concepts of highness and lowness, but in fact, God does not have highness or lowness.

89. *Biḥār al-Anwār*, v. 66, p. 293, h. 23.

The point here is that as humans we initially have this comfort with such material concepts, and when we want to think about immaterial matters, like in the case of Almighty God and His attributes, we firstly use such concepts and then gradually start to remove these thoughts from our minds, in order to get to the reality of these immaterial concepts. This also applies to perceiving God's supremacy and greatness. Almighty God cannot be perceived by sight, and when we are not yet able to see with the eye of the heart, how can we then perceive God's greatness?

There is a narration in *Biḥār al-Anwār*,[90] where parts of it could be relevant to our discussion here. It is a narration about a woman by the name of Zaynab al-ʿAṭṭāra (Zaynab the perfumer). She sold perfume in Medina, and that is why she became famous by the name of al-ʿAṭṭāra. Occasionally, she would go to the house of the Messenger of God (ṣ) and he or women in his household would purchase perfume from her.

One day, the holy Prophet (ṣ) entered his house, and there was a scent of perfume that had encompassed the area. He thought it must be Zaynab al-ʿAṭṭārah, and when he saw her, he said: "Whenever you come to our house, the house is filled with a pleasant scent." Zaynab al-ʿAṭṭārah, being the polite woman she was, replied: "O Messenger of God (ṣ) the scent of your presence is more beautiful than any perfume in the world, and the fragrance in the house is from your scent." She then said to him: "O Messenger of God (ṣ) today I did not come to sell perfume, but rather to discuss something with you." The Prophet (ṣ) said: "What is your question?" Zaynab said: "I came to ask you how can I know how great God is?" In reply, the Prophet (ṣ) said: "Think about the greatness of God's creation."

---

90. The whole narration can be found in: Mullā Muḥammad Ṣāleḥ Māzandarānī, *Sharḥ 'Uṣūl al-Kāfī* (Beirut: Dar Iḥyā' al-Turāth al-ʿArabī, 2000) vol. 12, pp. 167–168.

As Zaynab was in the beginning of her path, she was not able to perceive God's greatness with the eye of her heart. Her mind was still accustomed to material concepts, and she did not have the criterion to use to compare with immaterial things other than by those material concepts. This is why she had to start with physical and material concepts to comprehend metaphysical and immaterial concepts in order to ultimately reach perceiving God's greatness.

In regard to the greatness of physical entities, we are also limited as well. For example, if we wanted to comprehend how great Mount Damavand[91] is, we have no means other than to look at it from a far distance, such as in an aeroplane. Due to how large it is, if we were to look at it while being on the mountain, we would see it to be limited, and only see it from our specific side.

As a result, to view the mountain from all sides, we would need to be hundreds of metres above sea level and observe it from above. However, in this instance, Mount Damavand's true majesty won't be apparent to us, and we won't understand how great it is, because the farther we are from it, the smaller it appears to be to our eyes. When you're in the aeroplane, and you look at people or cars below you in the city, you see them to be way smaller than their real size.

We have this limitation in everything we perceive with our senses especially when it comes to large-sized things. This limitation also exists in our faculty of imagination perception as well. For example, if we wanted to imagine a great ocean, we would not be able to perceive how large it is without the external boundaries, or through our sense perception, even if our faculty of imagination was very strong, we would still not be able to go beyond how it exists externally, or maybe

91. Mount Damavand in Iran is a part of the Alborz mountain range. It is an extinct volcanic peak, the highest volcano in Asia, and the highest peak in Iran and Western Asia.

by just a little. This is what happens in the mind in giving physical boundaries to imagined things. It is for this reason that the size and largeness of great bodies cannot be perceived other than through sense perception, or even faculty of imagination.

After sense perception and imagination, the turn comes to rational perception. When we are unable to perceive via our senses and imagination the greatness of great and large bodies, we resort to the intellect and rational concepts. This is where comparison, relation and numbers come. For example, to explain the real greatness of the Mediterranean Sea, we say it is one million times larger than the beach we are imagining in our minds or perceive with our senses.

However, relying on this method of comparison and relation does not solve the primary problem, because for us, conceptualising numbers does not reach absolute, and in some cases the number will become so large it will be beyond our imagination. Furthermore, the real distance between numbers and relations are not clear within our mind. For example, we consider one hundred is ten tens, and one hundred million is ten sets of ten million. Here we have shown two relations between numbers, but there are ninety numbers that separate ten from one hundred, and then the distance between ten million and one hundred million is ninety million. There is a big difference between something being larger by ninety and something being larger by nine million, but our rational perception here says the difference in the two comparisons is just ten times.

Because of this, we are weak and lacking, even in our ability to comprehend magnificence and its material vastness. After giving these topics some thought, the first skill is to sharpen our perception of physical and material greatness and strive for more precision to recognise metaphysical and immaterial greatness.

I have given this relatively long introduction to discuss why in such narration the holy Prophet (ṣ) suggests this method to Zaynab al-ʿAṭṭāra, explaining to her the greatness of God's existence. If there was a land that spanned one hundred square kilometres, and your ring had fallen somewhere in this land, what would be the relation between the ring and the area of this land? Or, imagine the large Mount Damavand, and then put a ring next to it, what would the relation be between them? If you were asked, you would not be able to say that the ring has any significance in front of the land or the mountain. You would say it is so negligibly small, as if it is nothing. The Messenger of God (ṣ) guided Zaynab al-ʿAṭṭāra to this point, where if she wanted to perceive God's greatness, she must think about the greatness of God's creation.

The Prophet (ṣ) then said to her, describing God's greatness: "This earth, as great and large as it may be, is like a ring thrown into a desert." When compared to what encompasses it, it is like a ring in comparison to that very vast land. In this comparison, the ring is something very insignificant, or rather like nothing. After the Prophet (ṣ) made the comparison between earth and what encompasses it, saying that when it is compared to the first heaven, it is like "a ring thrown into a desert," he then told Zaynab that if you were to compare the first heaven with the second heaven, the first heaven will be like "a ring thrown into a desert". He continued to make this comparison until he got to the seventh heaven.[92]

At that time, they did not know about light years, and for a simple uneducated woman, nothing can be better than how the Prophet (ṣ) described the greatness of the world. In today's time, scientists and those who study space and astronomy can relatively conceptualise the relation this earth has to the solar system, perceiving how small

92. See: *al-Kāfī*, v. 8, p. 153.

our earth is. If we were to say our solar system is the size of an orange, earth would not be any larger than one of the holes in the outer skin of the orange.

The same is said when comparing the solar system to the Milky Way galaxy, which encompasses the solar system, and is nothing more than a straw in a large pile of hay. One light-second is equal to three hundred thousand kilometres, and the distance between Earth and the Sun is so vast that as fast as the Sun's light may be, it still takes approximately eight minutes to reach Earth.

This means that the distance between the Sun and Earth is about one hundred and fifty million kilometres. All this space with all that is in it, plus ten times more than what we have mentioned (which is the distance between the rest of the planets in the Solar System), when compared with how great the Milky Way is, the result is close to zero. Indeed, how great is the Milky Way, so much that millions of kilometres is regarded as nothing. Astronomers today say that the Milky Way is one of millions, or even billions of galaxies in the infinite universe.

At times, the distance between one galaxy and another could reach ten billion light-years. This means if we were to move at a speed of three hundred kilometres per second, we would need ten billion years, or three trillion nine hundred and fifty million days to reach another galaxy. Now, consider how small the earth is, and how insignificant it is when compared to this infinite vastness; it is something beyond comprehension. When a person compares himself to the Earth, he is like a straw, so how would he be when comparing himself to this universe? He would be like a black dot smaller than the tip of a pin in front of this infinite geographic vastness of existence. If we were to think deeply about this comparison, we would melt with so much shame and see how insignificant we are. Of course, Almighty God with one command brought this vast expansive world into existence, and with one command He is capable of making it non-existent.

Therefore, to understand one aspect of God's greatness, we should stimulate our minds the same way that the Prophet (ṣ) taught Zaynab al-ʿAṭṭārah, soaring over this vast infinite universe. We do hope that after decades of studying jurisprudence, principles of jurisprudence, philosophy and mysticism to be able to conceive the greatness of this world in the same level that this unschooled perfume seller had reached.

When commencing our prayer and saying *Allahu-akbar*, we must recall within ourselves how small and weak we are in the realm of existence and think of how insignificant we really are in front of this greatness. If we were to understand this reality, our outer and inner self would mirror a state of *khushūʿ* with no showing-off or pretending.

Without doubt, if we added other teachings to this, no existence that has all these weaknesses would show off its muscles in front of Almighty God, and never would disobey or declare war against Him. When realising these realities, if the human instinct was to awaken, even to the amount of a pinhead, the human would melt in shame and shyness, let alone wanting to face God with armour and fight Him. Along with perceiving God's greatness, if we were to take notice of the severity disobeying such greatness is, and the severity of punishment that awaits the disobeyers, our *khushūʿ* would increase manifold.

In summary, for us to attain *khushūʿ* in prayer, one way is to firstly think about how great God is. From the words of the holy Prophet (ṣ), to perceive divine greatness, we must think of how great God's creation is, and then focus on the point of He who created this great infinite universe with one command, how great is He! The greatness of

God is not physical or material, even though a way of understanding His greatness starts with material concepts and referents.

2. Looking at the Beauty of God's Attributes

Another way of achieving *khushūʿ* in prayer is to focus on the divine Attributes of Beauty (*ṣifāt al-jamāl*).[93] In reality, this method is one of intense yearning and love. When someone takes notice of the beauty of God's attributes, they will see God as a beloved existence who is worthy of praise and worship, and will therefore submit and show humility. This is a universal and general principle, that whenever a human loves someone, they will try more to get closer to them.

In regard to Almighty God, the deeper the heart loves God there will be a greater yearning to get closer to Him and connect to Him. Love of God is a result of knowing and recognising His Attributes of Beauty. Yearning to meet God will be more intense in the hearts of those who know and are better acquainted with the Attributes of Beauty of God, and the love of God will be deeper established in their hearts. If this state was to occur, even to a certain extent, one's prayer, which will become a time of meeting the Beloved, will become a cause for intensifying in the heart the yearning of connecting with Him. In prayer, when connection to the Beloved is made, one will feel humility and awe.

The origin of this state and its weakness or intensity corresponds to the level of how much one yearns to meet God. Meeting of God depends on the extent of how much one loves God, and love goes back

---

93. To simply put this, the attributes of Almighty God are usually divided into two categories, those of beauty (*jamāl*) and those of majesty (*jalāl*). The Attributes of Beauty are features that we affirm God as having, like knowledge, power etc. The Attributes of Majesty are features that we negate from God, like a partner, a body, etc.

to how much one knows God and His Attributes of Beauty. Based on this, even though one does not physically see his Beloved in prayer, but the flame of yearning to connect and the fire of the spiritual encounter takes over his complete existence.

3. Fear of God

Fearing Almighty God is also among the other factors that leads to *khushūʿ* in prayer. This has been explicitly mentioned and emphasised in many Quranic verses and narrations, saying that a believer must have a state of fear of God. In the Holy Quran, it says:

﴿فَلَا تَخَافُوهُمْ وَخَافُونِ إِن كُنتُم مُّؤْمِنِينَ﴾

So fear them not, and fear Me, should you be faithful.[94]

Almighty God also says:

﴿وَأَمَّا مَنْ خَافَ مَقَامَ رَبِّهِ وَنَهَى النَّفْسَ عَنِ الْهَوَىٰ * فَإِنَّ الْجَنَّةَ هِيَ الْمَأْوَىٰ﴾

But as for him who is awed to stand before his Lord and forbids the soul from [following] desire, his refuge will indeed be Paradise.[95]

And:

﴿فَلَا تَخْشَوْهُمْ وَاخْشَوْنِ﴾

So do not fear them, but fear Me.[96]

---

94. Quran, 3:175.
95. Quran, 79:40.
96. Quran, 5:3.

There are also many cases from the narrations of Ahlul Bayt (ʿa) that point to fearing of Almighty God to the extent that in some hadith compilations a separate chapter is dedicated to this topic of fear (*khawf*) and reverence (*khashya*) of God. There are many concepts in the supplications and prayers given to us from our noble Imāms (ʿa) that refer to this state of fear of God. For example, in the fifteen *munājāt* of Imām al-Sajjād (ʿa), there is the Munājāt of the Fearful (*al-khāʾifīn*).

In addition to all of this, the practical life of the holy Prophet and his Progeny (ʿa), and also righteous people all show the presence of a state of fear of God so much that in some cases they experience a kind of unconsciousness, as if they were overwhelmed due to how intense their fear of God was.

We must now investigate what is the meaning of "fear of God"? Is it possible that someone fears something or someone else, but also strongly connected to them with love and affection? In other words, is it possible that one feels pleasure in the fear of God? This question becomes more relevant in our time, where all are pursuing happiness, enjoyment, and entertainment more than fear, weeping or reverence.[97]

---

97. The concept of fear of God in the Islamic culture and in the Quran and Sunna, and encouraging towards it is something fundamental and cannot be denied. Certain people wish to present some weak misconceptions criticising and doubting this issue. For example, they say people should be fearful of scary existence, so is God a scary existence for us to fear Him? Clearly, this misconception comes from shallowness and naivety, and refuting it is very simple. To reply to this critique, we say that fear of God is, in reality, a result of our actions and comes from the system that Almighty God has placed regarding bad deeds. Almighty God has created the system of the world in such a way that whoever commits a bad deed, they will see bad effects, and when God resurrects us on Judgment Day, whoever has done bad will deserve punishment and be sent to Hell. This is the established system of existence, and because it is so, we fear that our deeds are bad and our wrongdoings will become a reason for us to be included in

We try to achieve *khushū'* in prayer, and one way of doing this is to gain a state of fear of God, and for this reason it is necessary for us to study the method of how to reach such a state.

Levels of Fear of God

1. Fear of Separating From the Lord

The first point to take notice of here is that there are different levels of people's fear of God, based on their level of faith and understanding, and it could be a very big difference. For example, the fear of the elite of God's saints is completely different from that of the fear that we have, and therefore the type of fear we have is not a kind of test for them. The Quran refutes them from having this kind of fear, along with mentioning their strong points and praiseworthy features:

﴿أَلَا إِنَّ أَولِيَاءَ اللَّهِ لَا خَوفٌ عَلَيهِم وَلَا هُم يَحزَنُونَ﴾

Look! The friends of Allah will indeed have no fear, nor will they grieve.[98]

Some of the supplications from Ahlul Bayt ('a), we can somehow deduce what kind of fear of God these great personalities had. For example, in the following part of Du'ā' Kumayl, Imām 'Alī ('a) beseechs Almighty God:

فَهَبْنِي صَبَرْتُ عَلَى عَذَابِكَ فَكَيْفَ أَصْبِرُ عَلَى فِرَاقِكَ

---

this system of retribution, and God forbid we earn Hellfire and His punishment. Therefore, Almighty God is not a scary dreadful entity, but the scary thing is our deeds and our wrong conduct that based on this system made by God that could result in Hellfire and divine punishment.

98. Quran, 10:62.

> Consider me.... if I patiently endure Your punishment, how can I endure being separated from You?[99]

What we understand from such statements is that the fear of God that the great men and women of religion have is by far more and stronger than our fear. They perceive the severity of divine punishment greater than us and they know its reality. They very well understand how severe and painful punishment in the Hereafter will be. However, they maintain that tolerating this punishment is easier for them than to tolerate being separated or distant from God.

We must indeed confess to the fact that we do not really understand the meaning of these concepts, because we do not feel anything absent when God is separated from us. In brief, if we were to get a bit closer to these issues, we must first understand the love relationship that brings together the lover and the Beloved. Those who know about the world of love know that the biggest need the lover has is to be the focus of their Beloved and to connect back to their Beloved in any way, shape, or form. The term that is opposite to separation (*firāq*) is connection or union (*wiṣāl*). If someone feels pain and wails from being separated from God, then they surely comprehend the meaning of union with Him.

Therefore, when the Commander of the Faithful (ʿa) said "if I patiently endure Your punishment, how can I endure being separated from You," it shows that he tasted the pleasure of connecting with the Almighty, because losing the connection and becoming separated will be followed by all this pain and punishment. Therefore, one must first become among the lovers to understand the meaning of "*wiṣāl*".

Those who live like this know that the relationship between the lover and the Beloved and everything involved in it creates a feeling

---

99. *Mafātiḥ al-Jinān, Dua Kumayl*

within them where no obstacle can come between them. This is the state of *wiṣāl*. In this state, each person will feel pleasure that cannot be described by words, all based on the level of love and existential perfection they have to their beloved. If we wanted to become familiar with this state, we must read *Munājāt of the Lovers* (*al-muḥibbīn*), from the Fifteen *Munājāt* of Imām 'Alī al-Sajjād ('a).[100] While pondering on its content, we are able to relatively gain closeness to what the Ahlul Bayt ('a) knew of divine love. Those who have reached the stage of loving God and tasted its sweetness will never feel anything else to be of importance. In *Munājāt al-Muḥibbīn* Imām 'Alī al-Sajjād ('a) says:

إِلَهِي مَنْ ذَا ٱلَّذِي ذَاقَ حَلاَوَةَ مَحَبَّتِكَ فَرَامَ مِنْكَ بَدَلاً

My Lord, who has ever tasted Your sweet love and then sought the love of another?[101]

Those who understand some of these meanings and have tasted its sweetness anticipate that their greatest wish is to gain that connection with their Beloved. Opposite to this, the worst thing they fear is to be deprived from this connection and suffer separation from Him. This is one type and level of "divine fear", and that is fear of separation and not accomplishing their hopes which they had gained some of its levels in this world, and the most complete level will be achieved in the Hereafter.

2. Fear of Being Deprived from a Glimpse of Divine Grace

Another level of fearing God is that of being deprived from the bounties of God in the Hereafter. The bounties of Almighty God can be universally divided into two types: material bounties and spiritual

100. *Mafātiḥ al-Jinān, Munājāt of the Lover*
101. *Mafātiḥ al-Jinān, Dua Abu Hamza al-Thumali*

bounties. Those who have reached complete recognition (*maʿrifa*) of Almighty God know that most of the spiritual divine bounties are God's attention and His caring of them. The most severe thing these people fear is to be deprived of these great blessings in the Hereafter, and that God will not accept them, not look at them and not talk to them. This is what we can see when Almighty God mentions the worst kind of punishment that will befall upon some people in the Hereafter, He says:

﴿وَلَا يُكَلِّمُهُمُ اللَّهُ وَلَا يَنظُرُ إِلَيْهِمْ يَوْمَ الْقِيَامَةِ﴾

And Allah will not speak to them, nor will He [so much as] look at them on the Day of Resurrection.[102]

These kinds of people have reached such a level of plight and degradation that on Judgment Day, Almighty God will not speak to them and not even look at them. Naturally, we are incapable of understanding how God's speaking or looking will be in that realm, and what this specifically means. Nonetheless, if we were to gain some of this worldly human love, we would know that there is nothing more hurtful for the lover than not being noticed or considered by the beloved. There is nothing more painful than being cut off and neglected by the beloved.

Even young children in this world would understand this. The most upsetting and hurtful thing for a child is for their mother to ignore and disregard them, and we can say this is applicable to adults as well. Those who have complete *maʿrifa* feel that Almighty God not talking to them and not noticing or looking at them is the most severe punishment. On Judgment Day, among God's severe punishments to the disbelievers and the disobeyers is that He will not look at them.

---

102. Quran, 3:77.

If it was not for such Quranic verses as the aforementioned, explaining these concepts would be very difficult, and so we use the Quran as a strong reference for these concepts. It is due to this that there are those who fear God that would disregard and overlook them. Of course, the general masses rarely take heed to this issue, or they naively think that God certainly loves them and without doubt will take care of them.

When those who have reached levels of high *maʿrifa* perform their acts of worship, all they want is for God to notice them. They wish at every instance they say "O God," they hear His reply "Here I am." One of the things the Infallibles (ʿa) would request in their supplications and *munājāt* is to hear a reply from Almighty God and gain His attention when they address Him and implore Him:

وَاسْمَعْ نِدَائِي إِذَا نَادَيْتُكَ وَأَقْبِلْ عَلَيَّ إِذَا نَاجَيْتُكَ.

And listen to my call when I call You, and attend to me when IwhispertoYou.[103]

There is no doubt that Almighty God is completely aware and knows everything and hears every sound, but this hearing is different, as it comes from love and attention. This does not necessarily mean that all of God's awareness comes from love and attention. We must distinguish between hearing and listening where at times we can hear someone say something, but we are also ignoring them and avoiding them. This kind of hearing is actually a form of punishment for the other person.

At other times, the hearing is also mixed with a smile and a glance from the lover to the beloved, and this kind of hearing gives the lover the highest excitement. The Infallibles (ʿa) in their supplications

103. *Al-Munājāt al-Shaʿbāniyyah.*

would ask Almighty God to grant them this kind of hearing. We also say such a thing when we are praying and raise our head from *rukūʿ*, saying *samiʿ Allah liman ḥamidah*.[104] When we say this, we want Almighty God to hear our praises and extolling of Him, and this hearing is one that comes from love and grace.

So, this is a type of "fear of God," where such people live in strong fear of not being blessed with God's concern, and not being addressed by God or be heard by Him. Loss of such divine attention is more hurtful for them than the torment of Hellfire. If a mother was upset with her child, that child would cry and beg the mother, saying: "hit me and do as you wish, but do not cut ties with me." Similarly, there are people who also say to Almighty God: "O God, burn me in Your Hellfire, but do not deprive me of a glimpse of Your attention." Their fear is to be deprived from a divine glimpse and being noticed.

As the Persian poet has said:

هر چه کُنی بکُن، مکُن ترک من ای نگار من

Do whatever you want to do, but do not leave me, O My Beloved.[105]

3. Fear of the Consequences of Sin

Another level of fear, which is a common type of fear, is fear of sin and its negative effects that encircle and envelop a person. This is the lowest level of "fear of God," and unfortunately due to our weak

104. This is recommended to say prayer, upon standing up after *rukūʿ*, and it means: God hears the one who praises Him.

105. This is from a poem authored by Muḥammad Taqī, and his pen-name was Shūrīde Shīrāzī (1857–1926). He had lost his sight at the age of seven due to smallpox and became so talented in poetry that he was given the title of The Most Eloquent in the Realm (*Faṣīḥ al-Mulk*).

ma'rifa and faith, we do not even take this low level of fear seriously. The Quran itself contains tens, or hundreds of verses that describe Hellfire and the punishments therein, and in some verses, we can see the broader descriptions of the punishment of Hellfire, like in the following verses:

﴿عَذابٌ أَلِيمٌ﴾

A painful punishment.[106]

﴿عَذابٌ عَظِيمٌ﴾

A great punishment.[107]

﴿عَذَابٌ مُهِينٌ﴾

A humiliating punishment.[108]

Other verses give details of these kinds of punishments, but have we ever thought to give ourselves time to ponder on these verses when we recite them? If we recite the Quran occasionally, we realise that we quickly read through the words and verses, just wanting to finish as quickly as possible.

When we hear a reciter with a nice voice, we focus on the technical skill the reciter has, whether he is good, has long breath, observes the rules governing pronunciation during recitation of the Qur'an (*tajwīd*), and we do not really pay attention to the verse itself, nor its meanings and content. Narrations aside, if we were to look at

106. Quran, 2:10. There are forty six places in the Quran where such an expression has been used.

107. Quran, 2:7. There are fourteen places in the Quran where such an expression has been used.

108. Quran, 2:90. There are eight places in the Quran where such an expression has been used.

the details mentioned in the Quran about Hellfire, it would not be a surprise that we somehow become similar to being insane.

The details and specifications mentioned in narrations about divine punishment are vastly more astonishing, but we also go through them and not take them seriously at all. One narration says that if one drop from the liquid drank by the dwellers of Hellfire was to be mixed with the water of Earth, all the inhabitants of Earth will die from its putrefying smell.[109] If we were to take notice of these concepts and see these punishments that we deserve because of insolence and sin, it would affect our fear and our awe of God.

In addition to the punishment for the sin, we must also pay attention to the evil of the sin itself and the severity of disobeying Almighty God. If someone was to disobey God even only once in their life, it would still be something very bad, and the person must be ashamed of himself. He is the Lord who is the reason for our very existence that we are disobeying. It is He who is the source of all these bounties that we are blessed with. When He orders us or prohibits us, it is for our own benefit but instead of thanking Him for that, we raise up our flag of insolence!

Almighty God says to us if we disobey Him, we make His and our enemy happy, but yet we still do it, and we make our and God's enemy happy. Opposing God's commands and prohibitions is nothing other than worshipping and obeying Satan, that Satan that is the enemy of the human being:

---

109. *Biḥār al-Anwār,* v. 8, p. 280, h. 1. The narration is: Imām al-Ṣādiq (ʿa) narrates from the holy Prophet (ṣ) who had said:
لَوْ أَنَّ قَطْرَةً مِنَ ٱلضَّرِيعِ قَطَرَتْ فِي شَرَابِ أَهْلِ ٱلدُّنْيَا لَمَاتَ أَهْلُهَا مِنْ نَتْنِهَا
If one drop from the poisonous thorny-plant of Hellfire (*ḍarīʿ*) was to fall in the water of the inhabitants of this world, everyone would die from its putrefying smell.

﴿إِنَّ الشَّيطانَ لِلإنسانِ عَدُوٌّ مُبِينٌ﴾

Satan is indeed human being's manifest enemy.[110]

Imagine one of your friends says to you: "Do not listen to what so and so says, because he's my enemy". If you were to listen to what your friend's enemy says, would you not be embarrassed to face your friend? Mind you, this friend of yours has not given you existence, sustenance, honour, status, or anything else; his status is just that of a friend. So, should we not treat Almighty God with the least level of how much we treat a normal friend?

Every sin we commit is obedience to our enemy and God's enemy. Almighty God has given us a set of commands that are a source of mercy and grace for us, so that we do not fall or be inflicted with problems, calamities, or difficulties. In this instance, we are rejecting divine love, and obeying our enemy and God's enemy. Indeed, how bad is this opposition! If someone was to just disobey God once, they would deserve to forever be deprived of His mercy, and for God to abandon them. If someone was to take one unlawful gaze at a non-maḥram person, God would have the right to take away their sight, because the Almighty gave the human eyes to use in the correct form, but instead we are using them in a harmful way. Does God then not have the right to remove our sight from us?

In one of supplications of Imām ʿAlī al-Sajjād (ʿa) , he says:

يَا إِلَهِي لَوْ بَكَيْتُ إِلَيْكَ حَتَّى تَسْقُطَ أَشْفَارُ عَيْنَيَّ ، وَانْتَحَبْتُ حَتَّى يَنْقَطِعَ صَوْتِي.... ثُمَّ لَمْ أَرْفَعْ طَرْفِي إِلَى آفَاقِ ٱلسَّمَاءِ اِسْتِحْيَاءً مِنْكَ مَا اِسْتَوْجَبْتُ بِذَلِكَ مَحْوَ سَيِّئَةٍ وَاحِدَةٍ مِنْ سَيِّئَاتِي

110. Quran, 12:5.

> O God, were I to weep to You until my eyelids drop off, or wail until my voice wears out.... And I do not lift my glance to the sky's horizons in shame before You, yet I would not merit through all of that the erasing of a single one of my evil deeds![111]

Imām al-Sajjād (ʿa) is saying: O Lord, if I was to commit one sin, I would deserve to stay in this state for the rest of my life, and with all my weeping and acts of worship, I would not be able to reach a state where I deserve to have one of my wrongdoings erased, unless it is from Your Grace and Mercy.

If you were to say to one of your friends, or your child, or anyone that respects you: "Do not do that act," but they disobey you, you might forgive them once, twice or three times. However, if the disobeying reaches hundreds or thousands of times, how would you deal with it? You would never look at that person the same again. You would be furious and no longer have any more patience towards them. It is for this reason that in one of the supplications of Imām ʿAlī (ʿa), he says:

إِلَهِي أَعُوذُ بِكَ مِنْ غَضَبِكَ

O God, I seek Your protection from Your anger.[112]

From the very first sin we commit, we deserve to be deprived of God's blessings, so what is expected after the hundreds of sins we commit? If we were to think about these issues, we would notice how we need to be ashamed and fear the Almighty more. If we were to pay attention to our insolence and what we deserve in punishment

---

111. *Al-Ṣaḥīfah al-Sajjādiyyah,* [English version], Supplication no. 16.
112. This is a part of *al-Munājāt al-Shaʿbāniyyah* of Imām ʿAlī (ʿa). See: Ibn Ṭāwūs, *Iqbāl al-Aʿmāl,* v. 1, p. 401.

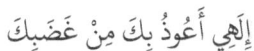

because of what we commit, we would break down in awe and humility.

Therefore, thinking about the sin, its punishments, realising who it is we are disobeying and sinning against, in how great He is, will increase how we see the severity of the sin and be more effective in creating a state of *khushūʿ*. We have some narrations that mention that one of the major sins is underestimating the severity of sin. If someone were to commit a very small sin, and they believe that it is not important at all, this would be considered as a major sin, worse than the sin itself. Not taking a small sin seriously, could result in it becoming a major sin because it shows one's carelessness in revering Almighty God and belittling His commands and prohibitions. This itself is a greater sin, and we must be cautious to avoid being afflicted with this sin.

If we were to correctly conceptualise this, it will result in the emergence of a level of awe we have towards the Almighty, and this will reveal itself in our prayer and form a state of *khushūʿ*. From another perspective, if our prayer is accompanied with *khushūʿ* it will certainly compensate for many bad acts and disobedience that we have committed towards Almighty God. There is a narration that says God will not punish the eye that weeps from fear of Him. As a result, even if the sins we commit have negative and harmful effects, turning to God in fear and reverence will, conversely, have positive results. It is for this reason that fearing God is a praiseworthy and good trait that is valuable and positive. During the night when Imām ʿAlī (ʿa) would worship, he would weep and say:

آهِ مِنْ قِلَّةِ ٱلزَّادِ وَطُولِ ٱلطَّرِيقِ.

> Alas! My provisions are scarce and the distance is long.[113]

What is someone like Imām ʿAlī (ʿa) really fearing? If he is worried about having a shortage of provisions, then what would someone like us do? The reality is we must admit that we have no idea about the realm in which Imām ʿAlī (ʿa) lived in . We must acknowledge that we cannot comprehend it, but we can only try to somehow get close to that state and imitate them.

The conclusion is that one of the effective ways of acquiring *khushūʿ* is prior to commencing prayer, we should think about how bad sins are and the negative consequences they have. Those who are familiar with the supplications and *munājāt* of our Imāms (ʿa), and frequently recite them will gradually transfer into a state of it becoming a fixed disposition (*malaka*). The result of this state is they will no longer need to sit down for an hour prior to every prayer and think about these issues. Once prayer time comes, or once they head towards the mosque, their state is transformed. When they hear the call "*qad qāmat al-ṣalāt*," they realise who they are going to be meeting with, and their state changes, becoming overwhelmed with *khushūʿ*.

---

113. Nahj al-Balāghah, Saying 77.

Chapter Four

On the Doorstep of the Beloved

The Role of Intention in Human Elevation or Fall

According to Quranic verses and narrations, prayer is the most important duty a human being has towards his Lord. Prayer exists in all divine religions, and all these divine religions have given importance to prayer over everything else, because of the effect this sacred act has on one's happiness, perfection, and spiritual elevation.

The concept of intention (*niyyah*) holds a critical position in acts of worship. Intention is considered to be the spirit of every act of worship, to the extent that the value of worship is completely connected to the intention of the worshipper. If intention was incorrect, as large as the act of worship may be, it would not bring any benefit to the person performing it. We also give intention great importance in our common daily activities in our life, and we believe that actions become of value and importance when they are done with the correct motive.

For example, if a friend while asking about ourselves uses certain expressions like "I love you", "I miss you", and we know these words genuinely come from their love and affection, we would consider the words to carry a very high value for us. It would also lead to an increase of our love and respect for that person as well. However, if we knew that these expressions came from deception and trickery, this showing of love and the words will have no value at all. In fact, if such words are repeated, it will become disturbing and repulsive for us.

Although these two cases on the surface seem to be the same, their intentions cause us to judge them very differently. What would we do if someone performed certain behaviours for us that show respect and consideration for our honour, but we knew that their only intention was to impress us? Not only would we see it to have no value, we would see it to be exactly the opposite of what they are doing.

Therefore, this is a general principle we see when rational people want to evaluate certain actions - they would not suffice only by looking at the outer act. They would also carefully examine what their intention was behind the act. Of course, specifying for every act what percentage we give to the value of the intention, and what percentage we give to other acts, this is a vast topic and will lead us away from our primary topic here, which is prayer.

Prayer can become a reason for spiritual elevation and reaching the highest stages and levels that are difficult for us to even comprehend. Many of God's saints have reached stations through prayer that cannot be described, and this is a reality that cannot be denied.

It is narrated that:

اَلصَّلاَةُ مِعْرَاجُ اَلْمُؤْمِنِ .

Prayer is the ascension of the believer.[114]

114. *Biḥār al-Anwār*, v. 79, p. 303, ḥ. 2.

The question here is to where and what level can prayer elevate us? The simple answer is: the levels of ascension that one can achieve through prayer are infinite. From another angle, prayer that is considered as an ascension could also lead someone to the lowest level of Hell. These two contradictory effects for one act are due to having two different intentions. An intention for prayer could result in the person elevating to the Realm of Dominion (*al-malakūt*), or it could also result in the person falling to the bottom of Hell. Imām al-Ṣādiq (ʿa) was asked about eternality in Heaven and Hell, and he said:

إِنَّمَا خُلِّدَ أَهْلُ ٱلنَّارِ فِي ٱلنَّارِ لِأَنَّ نِيَّاتِهِمْ كَانَتْ فِي ٱلدُّنْيَا أَنْ
لَوْ خُلِّدُوا فِيهَا أَنْ يَعْصُوا ٱللَّهَ أَبَداً وَ إِنَّمَا خُلِّدَ أَهْلُ ٱلْجَنَّةِ
فِي ٱلْجَنَّةِ لِأَنَّ نِيَّاتِهِمْ كَانَتْ فِي ٱلدُّنْيَا أَنْ لَوْ بَقُوا فِيهَا أَنْ
يُطِيعُوا ٱللَّهَ أَبَداً، فَبِالنِّيَّاتِ خُلِّدَ هَؤُلَاءِ وَهَؤُلَاءِ، ثُمَّ تَلَا قَوْلَهُ
تَعَالَى: قُلْ كُلٌّ يَعْمَلُ عَلَىٰ شَاكِلَتِهِ. قَالَ عَلَىٰ نِيَّتِهِ

> The people of Hell will dwell eternally in Hell because their intentions in this world were such that if they were to remain in this world forever, they would disobey God forever. The people of Heaven will dwell eternally in Heaven because their intentions in this world were such that if they were to remain here forever, they would obey God. Therefore, it is according to their intentions that these people and those people will have everlasting abodes.

He then recited the following verse: "*Say, 'Everyone acts according to his character*,'"[115] and said: This means according to their intention.[116]

---

115. Quran, 17:84.
116. *Al-Kāfī*, v. 2, p. 85.

Intention could have this level of effect in the action. Therefore, intention is the criterion to assess the value and the foundation of the spirit of worshipping. It is very important for us to think about the intention upon which the act of worship is initiated.

With exemption of acts of worship in the technical meaning, the importance of intention and its role in actions could be such that through intention we can make all our deeds acts of worship. Even things like eating, drinking, sleeping, resting, permissible entertainment and anything else can be forms of worship. Of course, this occurs when our goal for all these acts is to please Almighty God, so whenever we intend to do something, we do it with the intention to please God, that act will become an act of worship.

Obviously, specific acts of worship are different to other actions in that if we were not to have the intention of wanting to please God in our other actions, there would be no problem and it would not result in us becoming among the dwellers of Hell. However, for specific acts of worship, like fasting and praying, if we did them with the intention of showing-off, then these acts will result in us ending up in Hell.

In the specific case of prayer, we must put an emphasis again on how important it is to be very sensitive towards the intention. If the intention is right, the prayer will become a precious gem that will raise the person performing it to the highest level of Divine proximity, closer than any human heart can fathom. On the other hand, if, God forbid, the intention in our prayer is corrupt, this precious gem will not only lose its value, but will change into a harmful element, taking the person performing it to the lowest level of Hell. We implore the Almighty to grant us success in having all our acts of worship done with sincerity, especially our prayer.

Intention and its Levels

We have come to know that intention is the spirit of worship, and in general the value of any act goes back to its intention. We pointed to the fact that with some acts of worship, like prayer, if its intention is corrupt, like for showing-off (*riyā'*) or to win praises (*sum'a*), the act will not only have no effect and be invalid, it will also result in punishment.

At times, the expression "wholeheartedness" (*khulūṣ*) is used in opposition to showing-off (*riyā'*), and the Holy Quran uses other expressions as well, like "for the sake of God" (*wajh-i-Allāh*) and "seeking God's satisfaction" (*ibtighā'-a marḍāt Allāh*). We read in the Holy Quran:

﴿إِنَّمَا نُطْعِمُكُمْ لِوَجْهِ اللَّهِ لَا نُرِيدُ مِنكُمْ جَزَاءً وَلَا شُكُورًا﴾

We feed you only for the sake of Allah. We do not want any reward from you, nor any thanks.[117]

The expression *ibtighā'-a marḍāt Allāh* has been used in numerous places in the Quran as well, like:

﴿وَمَثَلُ الَّذِينَ يُنفِقُونَ أَموالَهُمُ ابتِغاءَ مَرضاتِ اللَّهِ﴾

The parable of those who spend their wealth seeking Allah's pleasure.[118]

It might be that this expression "*seeking God's satisfaction*" has a clearer meaning than the other two (*khulūṣ / wajh-i-Allāh*), and it

117. Quran, 76:9.
118. Quran, 2:265.

means that we are performing this deed so that God can be satisfied and pleased with us. For us the concept of satisfaction and pleasing (*riḍā*) is a mental state that we perceive through knowledge-by-presence (*al-ʿilm al-ḥuḍūrī*). When we are pleased with someone's action, we feel a state of happiness and contentment. So for the case of Almighty God, when He is pleased, does he go through a state of happiness and contentment because of our actions? We might find after completing this discussion that even though at first glance this expression of *seeking God's satisfaction* seems to be clearer than the other two expressions, it is not literally the case.

There are other expressions most jurists use when they say the act of worship must be performed "*with the intention of implementing God's command*" (*qaṣd al-imtithāl*). This means we perform an act because God has commanded us to do so, and we do it to obey His command. Of course, command (*al-ʾamr*) is broader than obligation (*al-wujūb*) and recommendation (*istiḥbāb*).

In any case, even though this concept is relatively easy for us to understand, we are still left with another question, which is: what is the state that we must achieve within ourselves to say that we have performed this act "*with the intention of implementing God's command*"?

In other words, we frequently use the expression "for the sake of gaining nearness to God" (*qurbatan ilā Allāh*). For example, when we want to pray, we say "I am praying Fajr prayer *qurbatan ilā Allāh*". The term *qurbā* means gaining proximity and closeness, and accordingly the expression would mean that we are performing the act of worship for the sake of gaining closeness to God. However, what does "closeness to God" mean?

Is Almighty God in a certain place or direction for us to get closer to Him? Therefore, this means that this expression is also vague as well. Unfortunately, we do not have the opportunity to discuss this here, as our aim is to avoid extensive philosophical and theoretical explanations and focus only on useful matters that are of practical benefit.

Types of Intentions

One of the meanings of intention in worship is while performing the act the person doing it is paying attention to what it is they are doing, to prepare the correct grounds to present the following question: Is this act what the Sacred Religion wants me to do? Is Almighty God pleased with this act? Opposite to this state is if someone was to do something without an intention. One could ask is it possible for someone to do something without an intention?

The answer to this is that such a thing could happen, but very rarely. In normal circumstances when someone is alert and mentally stable, they would do everything with a motive and intention, but if they have fainted or are semi-conscious, like being half asleep or maybe even drunk, they do not completely comprehend what they are doing. This results in their action being based on having a motive or intention in their mind. In any case, if someone was to perform any act of worship in such a situation, like praying, then even if they did all the obligatory acts and observed all its conditions, but it was not accompanied with intention, the act would be invalid. This prayer would be similar to those performing acts in their sleep, and when they awake and are asked what they did, they would remember nothing.

Another situation for intention in worship is for someone to perform the act of worship for certain motives and worldly gains, like the prayer of the hypocrites during the era of the Prophet (ṣ). They accepted Islam only for the sake of protecting themselves, and so that outer Islamic laws are applicable to them as well (like inheritance, marriage, etc.). These hypocrites would perform the Islamic rituals and acts of worship to protect themselves and their wealth, along with enjoying all the other privileges and earnings. If it was not for these things, they would certainly not pray, and without doubt their prayer was invalid as well.

From another perspective, it is a clear and obvious matter that the underlying motivation of any person's actions is to gain benefit and repel harm. It is also naturally possible for people to have different perceptions of benefit and harm, where one person would think something benefits them, whereas another would see that as harmful. However, it is definitely the case that the drive behind any action is to gain benefit and avoid harm. The actions we do are either for the purpose of earning money, gaining respect and status in society, reaching a rank or position, or to avoid being penalised or punished.

This is also applicable to acts of worship, especially prayer. Those who worship God and pray, although in reality they intend to worship and obey God's command, but this does not mean the benefits of performing the prayer or harms of abandoning prayer are not a part of their motive and intentions. Some of these effects could be worldly, like experiencing that prayer has granted them an increase in blessings in their life or giving charity has repelled misfortunes.

The effects could also be for the Hereafter. We rarely see people praying and not having a desire for Heaven or, on the other hand, fear of punishment for not performing this deed that is decreed obligatory by God. Most people who pray do so because they know He will punish in Hellfire one who abandons prayer, and if Hell did not exist, most people would not pray.

Of course, there is no doubt that there are righteous worshippers who cannot be compared with other people in their prayers and worship. Not only do they have in their prayer no greed for Heaven or fear of punishment, but even if there was no Heaven or Hell, they would still not abandon worshipping God. In some of the statements mentioned from the Infallibles (ʿa), while they were addressing Almighty God, they would say: "O God, even if various calamities and misfortunes were to befall upon me, I would still not stop worshipping and obeying You." We must request from Almighty God and put all our effort, so our worship and obedience become close to this level.

Yes, most of our acts of worship and obedience are a result of wanting Heaven or fear of Hell, to the extent that if God did not create a Heaven or Hell, those who worship and obey would be very rare, maybe even non-existent. What we are discussing here is this type of worship. What is its ruling as far Islamic laws and teachings?

A Correct and Accepted Intention

According to some narrations, worshippers are divided into three groups:

1) The worship of the first group of people is considered as "worship of slaves" because a slave fears his master and owner, is very cautious of him and therefore obeys his commands. There are some who worship and obey God only out of fear of God and His punishment.
2) The worship of the second group is "worship of merchants", because when a merchant and a businessman wish to conduct a business transaction, they look at the profits and benefits they will get out of it. There are some who worship God with this kind of mentality. They count what they will get in return for

their worship, that they will be gaining such and such. They see that if they worship, they will be granted Heaven, and that is their motivation.

For this group, it is a business transaction – with their fasting, their thirst, their hunger, their prayer, and even their jihad when they put their life in danger for the sake of God. They do all of this because they know they will get something in return that is worth hundreds more in reward.

We can see the Holy Quran using this approach to encourage people to do good and obey God, like:

﴿يا أَيُّهَا الَّذينَ آمَنوا هَل أَدُلُّكُم عَلىٰ تِجارَةٍ تُنجيكُم
مِن عَذابٍ أَليمٍ ۝ تُؤمِنونَ بِاللَّهِ وَرَسولِهِ وَتُجاهِدونَ في
سَبيلِ اللَّهِ بِأَموالِكُم وَأَنفُسِكُم ذٰلِكُم خَيرٌ لَكُم إِن
كُنتُم تَعلَمونَ﴾

O you who have faith! Shall I show you a deal that will deliver you from a painful punishment? Have faith in Allah and His Apostle, and wage jihad in the way of Allah with your possessions and your persons. That is better for you, should you know.[119]

The Holy Quran also used the word business in this context, and in other verses the expression buying and selling was used as well, like:

﴿إِنَّ اللَّهَ اشتَرىٰ مِنَ المُؤمِنينَ أَنفُسَهُم وَأَموالَهُم بِأَنَّ لَهُمُ
الجَنَّةَ﴾

119. Quran, 61:10–11.

Indeed, Allah has bought from the faithful their souls and their possessions for paradise to be theirs.[120]

Therefore, from the Quran and narrations it can be understood that this type of worship is accepted, and that greed for Heaven or fear of Hell will not affect the wholeheartedness of the intention that is connected to the value of the worship. If someone was to reach this level and truly believe in Heaven and Hell, and also act on this basis, then it is not a low level.

Of course, what they should aim and aspire to achieve is the level of worshipping God only for the sake that He is God. It should be that if there was no Heaven or Hell, it would not dissuade one from obeying and worshipping Almighty God.[121] It may be that most of the famous narrations on this issue is the following narration from Imām ʿAlī (ʿa) where he says:

إِنَّ قَوْماً عَبَدُوا اَللَّهَ رَغْبَةً فَتِلْكَ عِبَادَةُ اَلتُّجَّارِ، وَإِنَّ قَوْماً عَبَدُوا اَللَّهَ رَهْبَةً فَتِلْكَ عِبَادَةُ اَلْعَبِيدِ، وَإِنَّ قَوْماً عَبَدُوا اَللَّهَ شُكْراً فَتِلْكَ عِبَادَةُ اَلْأَحْرَارِ

120. Quran, 9:111.

121. Another fourth group has emerged in our time who say that we do not worship God for Heaven or Hell, because this is the conduct of an opportunist. This group differs from divine saints who do worship God in that way because this group in principle do not even believe in Heaven or Hell or its existence. Naturally, their acts will not incur any of these issues, in receiving reward or being saved from punishment. This group say that narrations mention Heaven and Hell only for the sake of motivating people to adhere to these moral and human principles, but in reality, there is no Heaven or Hell.
If these people were to say we do not worship God out of fear, this is because they do not have any fear within themselves, and the reality is that they do not believe in God for them to fear or not fear.

> There is one group who worship God for a gain, and this is the worship of merchants. Another group worship God out of fear, and this is the worship of slaves. Then another group worships God in gratitude to Him, and this is the worship offreemen.[122]

3) As for the worship of the free, it is those who have freed themselves from the limitations of Heaven and its bounties and Hell and fear of punishment. They are ready to endure all types of hardships and punishments of the Hereafter if that was to please Almighty God. The only thing important for them is God being content with them and gaining His love.
4) In a part of Ḥadīth al-Miʿrāj, it says that while the believer's soul is ascending towards the Throne, it says:

وَعِزَّتِكَ وَجَلاَلِكَ لَوْ كَانَ رِضَاكَ فِي أَنْ أُقْطَعَ إِرْباً إِرْباً وَأُقْتَلَ سَبْعِينَ قَتْلَةً بِأَشَدِّ مَا يُقْتَلُ بِهِ ٱلنَّاسُ لَكَانَ رِضَاكَ أَحَبَّ إِلَيَّ

> (I swear) by Your Might and Majesty, if pleasing You meant that I be cut up into pieces and be killed in seventy of the severest ways in which people are killed, having Your contentment would be more desirable for me.[123]

It is very easy to say such words but acting upon it is not something any person can do. If someone was to undergo a certain punishment only for an hour, they will then understand how severe this statement is. In Duʿāʾ Kumayl, Imām ʿAlī (ʿa) says:

122. *Nahj al-Balāghah*, Wise Sayings 234.
123. *Biḥār al-Anwār*, v. 74, p. 27, ḥ. 6.

فَهَـبْنِي يَـا إِلَهِي وَسَـيِّدِي وَمَـوْلاَي وَرَبِّي صَبَرْتُ عَلَى عَذَابِـكَ،
فَكَيْـفَ أَصْبِرُ عَلَى فِرَاقِـكَ

Then suppose, My God, my Master, my Protector and my Lord that I am able to endure Your punishment, How can I endure separation from You?

It is possible to read this statement as being said poetically, but there is no doubt that Imām 'Alī ('a) spoke it from the depth of his heart and with genuine truthfulness. Imām 'Alī ('a) believed that being distant from God is the most hurtful and most severe of any punishment.

Those who have experienced various types of strong and deep love know how pleasing the beloved affects the person and what they do. A lover would be willing to spend the whole night standing on his feet in the freezing cold weather to gain a smile or glance from his loved one. That very smile or glance would remove all the exhaustion and pain from that long night of standing outside. God's saints know that their Beloved will be pleased with them, so enduring all types of hardships and punishments for them is easy, even if it was punishment of Hellfire.

A Practical Step Towards Correcting Intentions

Thus far, we have discussed the importance of elevating our knowledge and awareness of prayer, and we have referred to some narrations that mention the importance of prayer. However would it be enough for us to just read books authored on the topic of prayer and worship? or read narrations that say:

الـصَّلَاةُ خَيْرُ مَوْضُـوعٍ، فَمَـنْ شَـاءَ اسْـتَقَلَّ، وَمَـنْ شَـاءَ اسْـتَكْثَرَ

Prayer is the best thing, so whoever wishes to do less can do so, and whoever wishes to do more can.[124]

Or,

اَلصَّلَاةُ قُرْبَانُ كُلِّ تَقِيٍّ

Prayer for every righteous person is a means of attaining closeness to God.[125]

Would it be enough to read such narrations for the purpose of performing recommended prayers and having sincerity in prayer and giving more value to it? There are many people who know about the importance of prayer and its status, and have heard many narrations about prayer, and how it should be conducted and its many merits. They know how valuable and important recommended prayers are, especially night prayers. They know how effective prayer is to one's happiness and success, yet with all this, they fall short and do not perform supererogatory prayers, especially the night prayer. It is for this reason that simply knowing, or reading is not enough, and one must also create fertile grounds within themselves to perform acts of worship sincerely for God, benefitting from any opportunity that would allow one to deepen their level of servitude to the Almighty.

We find that when a student or university undergraduate studies the whole study year to pass and get good grades, and to achieve this they may have to stay awake all night preparing for an exam the next day. For us, although we know the importance and value of prayer, we

---

124. *Biḥār al-Anwār,* v. 79, p. 307, ḥ. 9.

125. *Biḥār al-Anwār,* v. 78, p. 307, ḥ. 41.

are still not prepared to spend a few minutes of our time to perform recommended prayers, as easy as they may be.

It could be that the initial reply given by any person who stops short of fulfilling recommended prayers and not caring about prayer is that Satan has influenced them into not doing recommended deeds or from correctly benefiting from worshipping Almighty God. However, we must go through a psychological analysis of this issue to understand the real reason behind our neglecting or minimal interest in spiritual matters, among them being prayer. If we know that prayer is the best of deeds and the most profitable of trades, and in this transaction, we are not spending more than a few minutes of our time to get nearer to God, which is incomparable in its value to anything else, then why don't we do more of this profitable trade?

Someone clearly does not do something only for the purpose of benefit or profit, but studies all the aspects and defines all the harms and difficulties as well, along with the related consequences. After this, they look at the profits and benefits and compare them with the expenses, and if there is more profit and benefit, they proceed with the transaction. As for the case of performing a few rak'as of prayer, we certainly don't endure extreme hardships or difficulties, and in principle whatever we endure in the tiresome or difficult effort in prayer cannot be placed in front of the greatness and value of what we get back in return. So, why don't we do it?

The answer here is obvious, and that is the common habits in the behaviour of individuals is what prevents them from performing important spiritual deeds and worshipping God in its rightful way. We have gotten used to certain pleasures in our lives, and that is why we ignore doing anything that would oppose these pleasures. We have become habituated to being comfortable, and idle, and sleeping, and gotten used to these shallow worldly things.

Although one might not compare these habits to the reward that they could get through praying, abandoning these habits proves difficult. It is for this reason that short-lived temporal pleasures would prevent one from performing these important and valuable actions. Daily habits also obstruct acquiring a sincere intention in worship as well, or an increase in our attention to God. These habits are instruments of Satan that through them prevent us from reaching salvation and happiness. Therefore, we must focus on these habits that are an obstruction between us and the performing of important and beneficial actions, and that we distance them from ourselves.

The first step on this path is to become acquainted with the teachings related to the benefits that influence removal of useless shallow habits, and performing acts of worship with deeper servitude to God and gaining sincerity in one's actions.

The second step is "combatting the self" (*mujāhadah al-nafs*), i.e. the long bitter struggles against the self, and fighting against the habits of debased carnal worldly affairs. For example, even though excessive sleeping leads to laziness and is very harmful for someone, some people have become accustomed to it that they refuse to get out of bed before sunrise to perform their morning prayers. This bad habit of theirs prevents them from performing their obligatory duty, and if they wish to gain spiritual levels, they must face this habit and give preference to night prayers and morning prayers in their recommended times over the pleasure of sleeping.

Some are used to over-eating and filling their stomach with food, devouring whatever they feel. Of course, this vice of gluttony becomes a cause for many problems and hinders one from performing many important things. It is therefore necessary to confront these issues and try to eat and drink only what is essentially useful, and to avoid excessiveness and waste in eating and drinking.

The second stage of acquiring genuine intention and having sincerity in worship lies in fighting bad worldly habits. Of course, this fighting and jihad is indeed very difficult and needs a strong level of jihad and perseverance, and planning as well, especially when one grows older and facing these habits and traits becoming even more difficult.

For the youth, the habits that have yet to become strong and deeply rooted within them, opposing and combating them would not be that difficult. It is when habits become firmly rooted within oneself that they become very difficult. This is why the late Imam Khomeini in his Akhlāq lessons was very much focused on addressing the youth. He would say:

My dear, you must know the value of youthful age, and while you are young you should get up and worship and build your *self*, because once you reach old age, this success will be taken from you.

At that time, we did not really understand what Imam Khomeini meant, and we could not differentiate between an old person and a young person in the area of worship and self-building. Now we know that as long as one is young, the potential and success the youth can engender within themselves is vast, but when the same youth becomes old, he or she will be deprived of that.

In brief, in order to build ourselves and gain genuine intention in our prayer, to worship God as He deserves, in addition to paying attention to the obligatory prayers and praying recommended prayers, we must also aim at gradually cleaning out intention from any non-Divine impurities. We must get rid of the imperfections of showing-off (*riyā'*) and anything that leads to polytheism, making the intention sincere and deepening it to pave our way in reaching the highest levels of devotion to Almighty God.

We must benefit from these two elements while journeying on this hard and difficult path:

The first is acquiring inner-knowledge and awareness, elevating them to understand the benefits of worship, especially prayer, along with knowing the harms of abandoning it. Scholars of jurisprudence and Akhlāq have dedicated much time explaining these things.

The second element is combating bad habits, like laziness, love of comfort, food, and other moral vices that have infiltrated into the human self.

Levels of a Lofty Intention

We have mentioned that the most distinguished quality of worship is one in which the worshipper is not desirous of Heaven or fearful of Hell, but this stage itself has many levels and states. Those who reach this stage are not all going to be on the same level, and this is why in narrations there are different expressions about it. In the narration we mentioned, Imām ʿAlī (ʿa) explained this to one group by using the word gratitude (*shukran*) when he said one group worships God "in gratitude".

In this type, there is no desire for Heaven or fear of Hell that makes them bow and prostrate. They worship God to thank Him for His blessings.

It is the spirit of thankfulness that moves them towards worship and obedience. For them, even if there was no Heaven or Hell, they would still not withdraw from worshipping God. It is their conscience that does not allow them to overlook all these divine blessings and not thank God for them. The spirit of appreciation and gratitude is something we feel when someone offers some services to us, and we honour whoever assisted us. Our human instinct will not allow us to not be thankful for their services.

The Holy Quran refers to this in the following verse:

﴿وَوَصَّينَا الإنسانَ بِوالِدَيهِ حَمَلَتهُ أُمُّهُ وَهنًا عَلىٰ وَهنٍ
وَفِصالُهُ في عامَينِ أَنِ اشكُر لي وَلِوالِدَيكَ إِلَيَّ المَصيرُ﴾

We have enjoined man concerning his parents: His mother carried him through weakness upon weakness, and his weaning takes two years. Give thanks to Me and to your parents. To Me is the return.[126]

The verse mentions in conjunction, thanking God and the thanking of parents, perhaps because humans at first understand the value of the actions and services of their parents more than any other action or service. They witness and experience it all firsthand, seeing how the mother tirelessly takes care of raising her children, staying up all night and enduring all the strenuous work and hardships. This child sees how the parent works all the time, in hot or cold weather, spending long exhausting hours for the sake of securing means of comfort for the family.

One would be totally ready to thank their parents, and so when a son or daughter is asked to thank their parents, they will easily accept to do so. If someone is ready to show gratitude and appreciation to their parents for what they did and their services, this spirit of thankfulness will gradually become stronger within themselves and turn into a fixed state. The result of this is that this person will be thankful and appreciative to anyone who offers any service to him, or grants him any blessing. When such a person notices that all blessings

126. Quran, 31:14.

come from God, and the greatest and highest of services come from God, they will turn to thank Him, the Almighty.

Another expression that has been mentioned in narrations in this regard is the word "love" (*ḥubb*).

In narration from Imām Jaʿfar al-Ṣādiq (ʿa), he says:

...وَلَكِنِّي أَعْبُدُهُ حُبّاً لَهُ.

...but I worship Him out of love for Him.[127]

If there is a connection of genuine love between two people, and it is a very strong connection, the lover would not even think about attaining a benefit from their beloved. It would rather be the opposite, as the lover would want to offer anything and do anything they can for their beloved, without even noticing for a moment whether they will receive any reward or recompense from their beloved. One of the necessities of true and strong love is that the lover does not take notice of himself and sees nothing in front of him other than his beloved, directing all their existence to conform with the beloved. In this kind of a relationship, the lover does not think about whether they will be punished, or Heaven, or Houries, but just fixated on the Beloved and pleasing Him.

There is also another expression used by Imām ʿAlī (ʿa) where he uses the word "worthy" (*ahlan*), saying:

مَا عَبَدْتُكَ خَوْفاً مِنْ نَارِكَ وَلاَ طَمَعاً فِي جَنَّتِكَ وَلَكِنْ
وَجَدْتُكَ أَهْلاً لِلْعِبَادَةِ فَعَبَدْتُكَ

127. *Biḥār al-Anwār*, v. 67, p. 18, ḥ. 9.

> I did not worship You because I am afraid of Your Hell, or out of greed for Your Heaven. Rather, I found You worthy of being worshipped, so I worshipped You.[128]

Imām ʿAlī (ʿa) sees nothing but God being worthy of worship. He is saying that if I do not worship You, who would I worship, and if my heart is not connected to You, then who would I love?

The Gradual Process in Completing the Intention

In any case, these are different levels and concepts appropriate for the level of comprehension for various believers. We must, however, start with the lowest level, and then gradually progress to higher levels. The first level here is fear of Hellfire, and we can see many supplications from the Imāms (ʿa) that address this. For example, in Abī Ḥamzah al-Thumālī Supplication, Imām ʿAlī al-Sajjād (ʿa) says imploring his Lord:

فَمَنْ يَكُونُ أَسْوَأَ حَالاً مِنِّي إِنْ أَنَا نُقِلْتُ عَلَى مِثْلِ حَالِي إِلَى قَبْرِي لَمْ أُمَهِّدْهُ لِرَقْدَتِي وَلَمْ أَفْرُشْهُ بِالْعَمَلِ اَلصَّالِحِ لِضَجْعَتِي وَمَا لِي لاَ أَبْكِي وَلاَ أَدْرِي إِلَى مَا يَكُونُ مَصِيرِي وَأَرَى نَفْسِي تُخَادِعُنِي وَأَيَّامِي تُخَاتِلُنِي وَقَدْ خَفَقَتْ عِنْدَ رَأْسِي أَجْنِحَةُ اَلْمَوْتِ فَمَا لِي لاَ أَبْكِي أَبْكِي لِخُرُوجِ نَفْسِي أَبْكِي لِظُلْمَةِ قَبْرِي أَبْكِي لِضِيقِ لَحْدِي أَبْكِي لِسُؤَالِ مُنْكَرٍ وَنَكِيرٍ إِيَّايَ أَبْكِي لِخُرُوجِي مِنْ قَبْرِي عُرْيَاناً ذَلِيلاً حَامِلاً ثِقْلِي عَلَى ظَهْرِي

> Who is then worse than I am when I, such being my case, will be taken to a grave that I have neither paved for my long stay nor furnished with righteous deeds for my extended

---

128. *Biḥār al-Anwār*, v. 67, p. 186, ḥ. 1.

abode, while I do not know what my destiny will be? And while I notice that my self is cheating me, and the wings of death are fluttering over my head. So, why should I not weep? I weep for my soul's departure from my body. I weep for the darkness of my grave. I weep for *Munkar* and *Nakīr* interrogating me. I weep for my coming out of my grave (on the Resurrection Day) naked, humiliated, carrying my burdens on my back.[129]

If someone was to believe in the grave, in Judgment Day and in the dangers, frights, horrors and punishments contained therein, this would be enough for them to continuously remember God and not consider disobeying Him. These many tortures and punishments have been referred to in the Holy Quran. For example:

﴿خُذُوهُ فَغُلُّوهُ ۝ ثُمَّ الْجَحِيمَ صَلُّوهُ ۝ ثُمَّ فِي سِلْسِلَةٍ
ذَرْعُهَا سَبْعُونَ ذِرَاعًا فَاسْلُكُوهُ﴾

[*The angels will be told:*] *'Seize him, and fetter him! Then put him into hell. Then, in a chain whose length is seventy cubits, bind him.*[130]

When this person in Hell suffers from thirst due to the extreme heat and fire, they will have nothing to drink other than oozing pus (*ṣadīd*) that will be boiling from how hot it is:

﴿وَيُسْقَىٰ مِن مَّاءٍ صَدِيدٍ﴾

He shall be given to drink of a festering fluid.[131]

And,

---

129. Imām 'Alī al-Sajjād ('a), *Du'ā' Abī Ḥamzah al-Thumālī*.
130. Quran, 69:30–32.
131. Quran, 14, 16.

﴿لَهُم شَرابٌ مِن حَميمٍ﴾

They shall have boiling water for drink.[132]

A look into Adhān

Thinking about the content and meaning of prayer and becoming acquainted with the spiritual elements of this divine act helps us perform our prayer in a better form. We will benefit more from our prayer as well, because with a better prayer our other acts of worship will also be accepted.

In our prayer, there are movements and actions, like standing, bowing, prostrating, sitting while we recite the tashahhud, along with different things we recite that can be divided into three types:

First type: the invocations (*adhkār*), like "*Allāhu-Akbar*", "*al-Ḥamdu-lillāh*" and "*Subḥān-Allāh*".

Second type: reciting from the Quran that is obligatory in the first and second unit, and that is Sūrat-al-Ḥamd and a second Sūrah.

Third type: The supplications that are said in the *qunūt*, in bowing, prostration, before commencing of prayer and after completing prayer, although these are not obligatory.

Magnification of God in the Adhān

Allāhu-Akbar

The statement of "*Allāhu-Akbar*" is among the invocations recited in prayer that is repeated more than any other[133] and of which prayer

132. Quran, 6:70.

133. Throughout the day, just with the five daily obligatory prayers, and

cannot commence without, or else the prayer would be invalid. Any person praying would repeat the takbīr six times in Adhān and in Iqāma four times. The opening part of prayer commences with takbīratul-iḥrām,[134] and it is recommended to recite it after each act in the prayer. It is also recommended to do takbīr three times with the finishing of the prayer. Finally, among the things done after prayer (*taʿqībāt*) is *Tasbīḥāt al-Zahrāʾ* in which takbīr is repeated thirty-four times.

Monotheism in the Adhān

Ashhadu an lā ilāha illā Allāh

The second part of Adhān and Iqāma is bearing witness to monotheism, saying the invocation "*Ashhadu an lā ilāha illā Allāh*". This testimony of God's Oneness was the primary slogan of the holy Messenger (ṣ) as he would say:

قُولُوا لاَ إِلَهَ إِلاَّ اَللَّهُ تُفْلِحُوا

Say there is no deity but God and you will have salvation.[135]

The Holy Quran, in various contexts, mentions that the fundamental slogan for all Prophets is the statement of Tawḥīd and the testimony of God's Oneness. In the Golden Chain Narration, the importance and status of this slogan of Monotheism was clearly outlined. When Imām ʿAlī al-Riḍā (ʿa) travelled from Madina to Marw [Khurasan], upon his

---

not counting the recommended prayers, it would be repeated three hundred and sixty times.

134. Different explanations are given as to the reason why it is called takbīratul-iḥrām. It could be because the person entering into prayer is entering into the sanctity (*ḥarīm*) of God, until they finish with taslīm, or that it will become a reason for whatever is usually ḥalāl outside of prayer, like eating and drinking, now becomes ḥarām while praying.

135. *Biḥār al-Anwār*, v. 18, p. 202, ḥ. 32.

arrival in Nayshabour, he quoted in the presence of a large number of scholars and narrators a report from his forefathers (ʿa), from the Messenger of God (ṣ), that Almighty God had said:

كَلِمَةُ لاَ إِلَهَ إِلاَّ اَللَّهُ حِصْنِي فَمَنْ قَالَهَا دَخَلَ حِصْنِي وَمَنْ دَخَلَ حِصْنِي أَمِنَ مِنْ عَذَابِي

The statement of *lā ilāha illā Allah* is My fort. Whoever utters it will enter My fort, and whoever enters into My fort will be safe from My punishment.[136]

A Fundamental Question

Many studies have been done about the reality and levels of monotheism, and of course it is not possible to present them here in this book, but it is important to answer a fundamental question about this, and that is:

What is so important about the statement of tawḥīd to the extent that it has been allocated in the beginning of prayer and in its obligatory parts? We testify to Tawḥīd twice in our Adhān, after the takbīr, then again at the end of Adhān, in Iqāma as well, three times, and in tashahhud we say "*Ashhadu an lā ilāha illā Allāh*" as well. From another side, we see the holy Prophet (ʿa) and the Imāms (ʿa) stressing this slogan, as can be seen in a narration from Imām al-Ṣādiq (ʿa) who narrates the following about his father Imām al-Bāqir as):

كَانَ أَبِي كَثِيرَ اَلذِّكْرِ لَقَدْ كُنْتُ أَمْشِي مَعَهُ وَإِنَّهُ لَيَذْكُرُ اَللَّهَ وَآكُلُ مَعَهُ اَلطَّعَامَ وَإِنَّهُ لَيَذْكُرُ اَللَّهَ وَلَوْ كَانَ يُحَدِّثُ اَلْقَوْمَ مَا يَشْغَلُهُ ذَلِكَ عَنْ ذِكْرِ اَللَّهِ وَكُنْتُ أَرَى لِسَانَهُ لاَصِقاً بِحَنَكِهِ يَقُولُ لاَ إِلَهَ إِلاَّ اَللَّهُ

136. *Biḥār al-Anwār*, v. 49, p. 127, ḥ. 3.

> My father would always recite invocations. I would walk with him and he would remember God, I would eat food with him and he would remember God. Even when he spoke with people, it would still not prevent him from remembering God. I would see his tongue attached to his palate, saying "there is no deity but God".[137]

So, we ask why is there this much focus on saying of *lā ilāha illā Allāh* and announcing the Oneness of God?

The general answer to this is that the reality of Islam is tantamount to Tawḥīd. The late ʿAllāmah Ṭabāṭabāʾī would say in this regard:

> If we were to combine all dimensions of Islam and bring them all together, our result would be the statement of "*lā ilāha illā Allāh*". If we were to dissect this statement, we would end up with all the teachings of Islam. Therefore, all the teachings of Islam are nothing other than the details of the statement of "*lā ilāha illā Allāh*".

It must be said though that conceptualising, understanding, and believing in this narration is also considered as something difficult for us, being that everything in Islam in all its branches of belief, morals, values and laws are all summarised in the statement of "*lā ilāha illā Allāh*".

The clear answer to this is that Islam outlines the direction of human life and method of gaining perfection. According to narrations, this is the "dye of God" (*ṣibghatullāh*),[138] as the Almighty says:

---

137. *Biḥār al-Anwār,* v. 46, p. 297, ḥ. 29.

138. See: *Biḥār al-Anwār,* v. 3, p. 280, ḥ. 15, and v. 64, p. 131, ḥ. 1. And p. 133, ḥ. 2.

﴿صِبغَةَ اللَّهِ وَمَن أَحسَنُ مِنَ اللَّهِ صِبغَةً﴾

The colouring[139] *of Allah, and who colours better than Allah?*[140]

This religion, brought by the holy Prophet (ṣ), the religion we believe in and consider acting upon it obligatory, worthy of millions of people sacrificing themselves for it, is defined as the necessary movement towards God in all aspects of a human's life. This means in one's behaviour, ideas, beliefs, morals, individual and social relationships, and that every decision and movement they take in all aspects of their personal or social life is towards Almighty God.

If we were to accept this understanding of our religion, that Islam directs humans towards absolute perfection and nearness to God, and that Islam is the guide in all parts of life, this reality would be clear for us, that the essence and purpose of Islam is nothing other than directing oneself to the One God.

What Islam came up with is either turning people to God directly or preparing the preliminaries to turn to God and become close to Him. All the laws and commands in the branches of Islam, even the obligatory and recommended laws that are related to one's carnal conduct and acts are for the sake of obtaining that "dye" of God and receiving the Godly direction. If this carnal behaviour takes a divine quality and pursues the path of obedience to God, gaining His satisfaction, then it will earn value.

Monotheism in Islam is the curing ointment that includes believing in God's Oneness, His Creation, His Lordship in creation

139. Some English translations have used the term baptism of God for *ṣibghatullah*, saying that Christians refer to the act of baptising as "*inṣabagha*", but the *ṣibgha* of God refers to the nature and instinct of the human being that God has created them with. (Tr.)

140. Quran, 2:138.

and His Lordship in legislation.[141] Monotheism is the cause of human happiness and elevation, and attaining happiness and elevation comes through accepting all aspects and pillars of monotheism. If someone does not accept one pillar of monotheism, it is as if they have not accepted the basis of monotheism. It is like having an ointment that lacks its fundamental ingredient, not only will it not cure, but it could also be harmful. The Almighty refers to this reality, saying:

﴿إِنَّ الَّذِينَ يَكْفُرُونَ بِاللَّهِ وَرُسُلِهِ وَيُرِيدُونَ أَن يُفَرِّقُوا بَيْنَ اللَّهِ وَرُسُلِهِ وَيَقُولُونَ نُؤْمِنُ بِبَعْضٍ وَنَكْفُرُ بِبَعْضٍ وَيُرِيدُونَ أَن يَتَّخِذُوا بَيْنَ ذَٰلِكَ سَبِيلًا ۝ أُولَٰئِكَ هُمُ الْكَافِرُونَ حَقًّا﴾

Those who disbelieve in Allah and His apostles and seek to separate Allah from His apostles, and say, 'We believe in some and disbelieve in some' and seek to take a way in-between. It is they who are truly faithless.[142]

A believer is someone who believes in the entirety of the religion. If someone believes in one part of the religion and rejects the other, they are in fact a disbeliever because they do not believe in everything that God has sent down. Furthermore, deep in their heart they still do not believe in God's religion, as they are worshiping their desires, and not really worshipping God, because they believe in that part of religion only because it suits them and their desires, and not because it is something brought down by Almighty God. Someone who really does worship God believes in everything He has sent down and does not follow their own desires and inclinations.

---

141. *Rubūbiyyah Takwīniyyah / Rubūbiyyah Tashrīʿiyyah*

142. Quran, 4:150–151.

The result of believing in the Creator and His Lordship in creation and Lordship in legislation is believing that God is the Creator of the world who oversees and manages it. God defines the laws and principles that secure the path to human happiness, and this is precisely where humans develop such motives for worshipping Him, because they know that God controls existence. They do not go towards anyone else to secure their needs, and they will ultimately never give in to their desires and inclinations. However, if they reject Lordship in legislation and do not accept God's laws, whether they admit it or not, they will be driven towards others, and ultimately submit their will and their desires in acknowledgment of the will of someone other than Almighty God.

If someone believes that God is their Creator and that creational Lordship, legislative Lordship and all existence are from God, they will have no path in front of them other than to submit to God. When one believes their existence is from God, what other power will they rely on other than God? When one knows that God oversees the entire universe, there is no meaning for them to turn to someone else (to fulfil their needs), because everyone other than God does not own anything they can give to this person. It is for this reason that believing in Tawḥīd – the slogan of Islam, and the *dhikr* of "*lā ilāha illā Allāh*" that explains this slogan is based on three foundations:

1. Believing in God's creativity (*al-khāliqiyya*).
2. Believing creational Lordship (*rubūbiyya takwīniyya*).
3. Believing in legislative Lordship (*rubūbiyya Tashrīʿiyya*).

These foundations lead to believing in devotion to God, and this is the slogan of Monotheism that Imām ʿAlī al-Riḍā (ʿa) referred to under the title of "God's Fort".

In conclusion, the statement of "*lā ilāha illā Allāh*" is not just words or a slogan. It represents a set of monotheistic beliefs that enter the heart of a monotheist. According to the firmly established doctrines, it makes this person believe that existence is solely related to God and He manages all affairs of the world, He secures all needs, and there is no one worshipped other than Him. Based on this, there is no meaning in turning to anyone other than God. This is why so much special attention and weight has been given to monotheism because strong belief in monotheism in doctrine, morals and legislation leads one to understand their whole existence coming from God, and they turn to God without any instance of inattentiveness.

Testifying to the Message in Adhān

Ashhadu anna Muḥammad Rasūllulāh

Along with believing in Tawḥīd, a Muslim must also believe in the Message (*al-risāla*) of the Messenger of God (ʿa), believing he brought this religion from God and submitting to His Legislation (*sharīʿa*). Naturally, bearing witness to the Risāla is dependent on the fact that Almighty God has sent a prophet and a messenger to convey His religion to us, which would also include legislation and divine law. After knowing that the person sent by God is the Messenger of God and the Seal of Prophets and we came to know his religion, we would then be committed to act upon everything he informs us of, due to it being revelation from God. We must accept everything he explains to us, because he is a Prophet, sent by God and he is the owner of the *sharīʿa*. We must acknowledge him, submit to his commands and laws, as obeying the Messenger of God (ṣ) is obligatory in relation to obedience to God. Testifying to the Prophet's Risāla is a component for faith in Islam and faith in God, which is why this testimony is a continuation and extension to the testimony of monotheism.

The Concomitance Between Believing in the Risāla of the Prophet (ṣ), Imāma and Guardianship of the Jurist

The Messenger of God (ṣ) is sent from Almighty God and he is the owner of the *sharīʿa*, ruling and guiding people, and his permission is God's permission, obeying everything he says and directions becomes obligatory. This means that obeying the Infallible whom the Prophet (ṣ) appointed is obligatory for us as well and believing in his authority is an extension and completion of believing in the Risāla.

The Infallible Imām is the Successor (*khalifa*) of the Messenger of God (ṣ) who gave the Infallible the authority, so obeying him is obligatory in continuation of obeying the Messenger of God (ṣ). Furthermore, obeying whoever the Infallible appoints, in general or specifically, is also obligatory. Therefore, obeying the Guardian Jurist (*al-walī al-faqīh*) is a reflection of obeying the Infallible Imām, which in turn is a reflection of obeying the Messenger of God (ṣ), which of course reflects obedience to Almighty God. It is for this reason that the faithful mention the following in their Adhān and Iqāma: "*Ashhadu anna ʿAlī-yan waliyullah*".[143]

With this explanation, we understand the importance of the Risāla and bearing witness to it, where testifying to the Risāla in Adhān and Iqāma is placed beside testifying to Tawḥīd. We also bear witness to the Prophet's Risāla in our tashahhud as well. An important point here is that in Islamic law if someone was to unintentionally miss something out in their prayer, in certain cases they can compensate

---

143. An important note believers know is that this statement is not said as a part of the Adhān or Iqāma, and as our esteemed jurists have said if someone was to consider it as a part of Adhān or Iqāmah, not only will it be invalid, they have also committed an innovation. Rather, as expressed by the late Grand Ayatullah Sayyid Muḥsn al-Ḥakīm, it is to be said as a slogan and symbol of Shīʿism.

that with performing *sajdatay al-sahw*[144] after their prayer. In this prostration, in front of the Grandeur of the Almighty, the *dhik*r to be recited is: "*Assalāmu alaika ayyuha al-Nabī-yu wa raḥmatullah-i wa barakātuh*". Prostration is an essential act of worship that cannot be done except for Almighty God, however, to compensate for a deficiency in the prayer, one must turn to the holy Prophet (ṣ) and send salutations to him.

Absolute Faith in the Message of the Seal of Prophets (ṣ) and Other Prophets

It is necessary to point out that believing in the legislative Lordship of God does not mean we are able to follow any legislation. We must emphasise this fundamental belief that after the commencing of the Mission (*bi'tha*) of the holy Prophet (ṣ), only he is to be obeyed, and we must not acknowledge any legislation except his, and therefore practicing any other legislation will not be accepted. Of course, we do believe that the legislations of other prophets were correct within their circumstances and conditions, and valid at their time. They are to be respected because it is obligatory for us to respect all other prophets and it is prohibited to insult any of God's prophets. Rejecting any of the legislations sent down by Almighty God is equal to rejecting all divine legislations.

The Holy Quran praised Abraham ('a), Moses ('a) and Jesus ('a), and the Quran affirmed their legislations, considering them correct and valid for the people of their time. The Almighty says:

144. *Sajdatay al-sahw* is an extra two prostrations performed after the completion of the prayer to make up for certain instances in prayer that were forgotten or incorrectly done.

﴿آمَنَ الرَّسُولُ بِمَا أُنزِلَ إِلَيْهِ مِن رَّبِّهِ وَالْمُؤْمِنُونَ كُلٌّ آمَنَ بِاللَّهِ وَمَلَائِكَتِهِ وَكُتُبِهِ وَرُسُلِهِ لَا نُفَرِّقُ بَيْنَ أَحَدٍ مِّن رُّسُلِهِ﴾

The Apostle has faith in what has been sent down to him from his Lord, as do men of faith. Each [of them] has faith in Allah, His angels, His scriptures and His apostles. [They declare,] 'We make no distinction between any of His apostles.'[145]

Therefore, a requirement of believing in God is not to make any distinction between any of God's messengers, and to believe and affirm all of them because it is obligatory to obey one who comes with a divine message. There were people in history who did not have faith, nor believed in what God sent down, and this is why the Almighty mentions:

﴿إِنَّ الَّذِينَ يَكْفُرُونَ بِاللَّهِ وَرُسُلِهِ وَيُرِيدُونَ أَن يُفَرِّقُوا بَيْنَ اللَّهِ وَرُسُلِهِ وَيَقُولُونَ نُؤْمِنُ بِبَعْضٍ وَنَكْفُرُ بِبَعْضٍ وَيُرِيدُونَ أَن يَتَّخِذُوا بَيْنَ ذَٰلِكَ سَبِيلًا ۝ أُولَٰئِكَ هُمُ الْكَافِرُونَ حَقًّا وَأَعْتَدْنَا لِلْكَافِرِينَ عَذَابًا مُّهِينًا﴾

Those who disbelieve Allah and His apostles and seek to separate Allah from His apostles, and say, 'We believe in some and disbelieve in some' and seek to take a course midway. It is they who are truly faithless, and We have prepared for the faithless a humiliating punishment.[146]

If someone was not to believe in any one of the approximately one hundred and twenty-four thousand prophets, they would be considered as a disbeliever and deserve punishment in the afterlife

145. Quran, 2:285.
146. Quran, 4:150–151.

because faith is absolute and cannot be partitioned. Someone not believing in all divine prophets and messengers is not a believer, and one cannot say they are entitled to Heaven and various degrees of faith based on the proportion of how many prophets they believe in. When discussing belief in monotheism, we said belief can only occur if someone believes in all levels and pillars of monotheism, which are Divine creation, creational Lordship and legislative Lordship. If not, they would be considered a disbeliever, due to an element of deficiency in their faith.

That is why Satan, although he believed in Divine creation and God's Creational Lordship, and also believed in Judgment Day, was dismissed and expelled from the divine realm of the Almighty to be considered among the disbelievers because he did not submit to the legislative Lordship of Almighty God. Satan did not adhere to God's command to prostrate to Adam, and Satan did not have absolute submission to God. Satan is considered among the leaders of Hell, and he will be the cause of others entering Hell because of his deception and misguidance of others. Satan believed in God being the Creator and His Creational Lordship, but because of his arrogance towards God, he became the vilest of disobeyers and the most tyrannical one.

As it is necessary to have absolute faith in God, the believer must also have faith in the messages of all the prophets, and if one was to reject any of the one hundred and twenty-four thousand prophets, it would be as if they have rejected all of them. This is because if their belief in prophets is not out of personal interest or desire, but because they are messengers and prophets sent by God, then they must believe in the prophet they decide to reject. He is a prophet and a messenger of God, and no distinction should be made between any of them.

The *Ḥayya'alāt*: The Three Parts of Adhān

We have briefly gone through the topic of monotheism and the testimony of God's Oneness and the Message. We will now discuss the three parts of Adhān and Iqāma and their relation with each other, and they are "hasten to prayer" (*ḥayya 'alā al-ṣalāt*), "hasten to salvation" (*ḥayya 'alā al-falāḥ*) and "hasten to the best deed" (*ḥayya 'alā khayr al-'amal*).[147] These statements are structured in the form of slogans and for public announcement. The *ḥayya 'alā al-ṣalāt* means rush and hasten towards prayer, *ḥayya 'alā al-falāḥ* means rush and hasten towards victory and salvation, meaning salvation is achieved through prayer. As for *ḥayya 'alā khayr al-'amal*, this also refers to prayer being the best of deeds.

Some Important Questions

In conclusion of this chapter, we now address some questions related to prayer and reply to them.

Question One: Seeing that Adhān was legislated as a public announcement and to inform those who pray to hasten in participating in congregational prayer, why is it still recommended to Adhān and Iqāma if someone is praying on their own and in privacy?

In other words, the expressions of "*ḥayya 'alā al-ṣalāt*", "*ḥayya 'alā al-falāḥ*" and "*ḥayya 'alā khayr al-'amal*" are public announcements to perform prayer, and if a person praying by himself would say them, who is he inviting to prayer?

Answer: Reciting these statements when praying alone is to dictate upon oneself and direct oneself to understand the status of prayer and

147. These three *dhikr*'s are referred to as the *Ḥayya'alāt*.

that prayer leads to victory and success. When the Adhān is called as a public announcement, it includes the person reciting it as well, by also inculcating and directing it to himself. It is not necessary that Adhān and Iqāma be addressed to other people. Reciting the Adhān and Iqāma is a public call and notifying people for prayer, but it is also for inculcating and directing one's self to the status of prayer and towards Almighty God whom the person praying will be standing in front of.

Question Two: In the case of "*ḥayya 'alā al-falāḥ*", which is a part of Adhān and Iqāma, is prayer itself salvation, or does prayer lead to salvation?

Answer: The Arabic word *al-falāḥ* (الـفلاح) was used in Arabic literature before Islam, but with the advent of Islam and with the vast use of this word in the Holy Quran, it turned into a key term in Islamic teachings. In line with this, Muslims followed the Quran by using this term frequently in their literature.

The Holy Quran frequently uses the word *al-falāḥ* and its derivatives. For example, the first verse in Sūrat al-Mu'minūn says:

﴿قَد أَفلَحَ المُؤمِنونَ﴾

Certainly, the faithful have attained salvation.[148]

And in Sūrat-al-Baqara, after Almighty God introduces the Godwary, He says:

﴿أُولٰئِكَ عَلىٰ هُدًى مِن رَبِّهِم وَأُولٰئِكَ هُمُ المُفلِحونَ﴾

Those follow their Lord's guidance, and it is they who are the felicitous.[149]

148. Quran, 23:1.
149. Quran, 2:5.

It is useful to mention here a relevant grammatical point, and that is that the verb (*afʿāl*) are usually transitive (*mutʿaddī*), but at times are not, and are used in the form of an intransitive verb (*lāzim*). An example for this can be seen in the previous two verses, where *aflaḥa* and *al-mufliḥūn* are both intransitives. The word "*aflaḥa*" means he has gained *falāḥ*, and "*al-mufliḥ*" means he enjoys *falāḥ*.

The word *falāḥ* is used in the meaning of winning (*al-fawz*) felicity (*al-saʿādah*) and victory (*al-intiṣār*), as mentioned in the following verse:

﴿وَقَدْ أَفْلَحَ الْيَوْمَ مَنِ اسْتَعْلَىٰ﴾

Today he who has the upper hand will win![150]

Here *aflaḥa* means winning and overcoming, as is also the following verse:

﴿وَلَا يُفْلِحُ السَّاحِرُ حَيْثُ أَتَىٰ﴾

And the magician does not fare well wherever he may show up.[151]

Therefore, the meaning of *falāḥ* is closely related to the concepts of "winning" and "victory", and this can be observed when examining cases of its usage. To further explain, every human being instinctively craves happiness, and we cannot find someone who does not search for happiness. If someone wants to search for happiness, they must first overcome the obstacles that hinder their path towards it, to get to their objective. If one reaches happiness, they will be successful as far as overcoming those obstacles and being saved from the elements that prevent them from reaching their objective.

---

150. Quran, 20:64.
151. Quran, 20:69.

The word *falāḥ* is used in this context, saying they have succeeded, which means that *falāḥ* means someone has overcome the obstacles that hinder their perfection and reaching their goal. In other words, they are saved from the obstacles.[152] However, if we were to take into consideration the person's arrival to their objective and happiness, then the word win (*fāz*) would be used in this regard, which means that this person has been successful in attaining their objective.

Therefore, prayer is an element of salvation, and in the Adhān and Iqāma, those who pray are invited to this prayer. The dhikr of "*ḥayya ʿalā al-falāḥ*" informs the person praying about this, where through praying they will reach salvation.

Question Three: Why does prayer lead to salvation?

Answer: In this life, material needs and attachments themselves alone do not assist a human being to reach happiness but rather they could be obstacles preventing them from attaining happiness. Our material needs and attachments can be seen from a very early age in our lives, where even an infant just born expresses their need for food by crying. Of course, this attachment continues to increase with time, until it gets to a level where one becomes attached to status, ruling, control, and worldly fame.

Among the primary needs for securing one's material needs and interests is the desire to attain them. This desire, other than being temporary, also brings a lot of exhaustion and hardship. For example, if someone were to eat something after feeling hungry, but exhaust themselves in securing this food, and even eating the food takes up effort. When finishing the food and becoming full, one feels lethargic and heavy, and this pleasure is restricted only to the time in which

---

152. It is for this reason that a farmer in Arabic is called a *fallāḥ* because he removes the obstacles that prevent growth of the seed.

the taste buds feel the taste of the food. It is noticeable how people pursue fulfilling this necessary need of the body to protect human life, so much so that if one was not to eat, they would die. How much do people endure in difficulties and hardships just to secure a short-lived pleasure for themselves, and this is the same for other material needs and attachments, always accompanied with suffering, excessive effort, enjoying limited and transient pleasure.

Now, as far as the human being's ultimate goal is getting close to Almighty God, and the path to Him is turning to Him and obeying Him, would consuming one's life and energy to achieve material gains, or engaging in either legitimate or illegitimate worldly contests, or many other problems lead to forgetting God and prevent gaining closeness to Him? In any case, there is no escaping from the necessities of this material life, as it chains down our hands and feet, preventing us from moving towards perfection and becoming closer to God.

If material attachments and their legitimate usage divert us from God, then what can be said about illegitimate usages, which of course lead to these shackles, blocking someone from getting to their destination. Furthermore, we know that Almighty God created the human being and made his goal to pursue ultimate perfection, i.e. getting close to God, which is the station He describes in the following verse:

إِنَّ الْمُتَّقِينَ فِي جَنَّاتٍ وَنَهَرٍ ۝ فِي مَقْعَدِ صِدْقٍ عِنْدَ مَلِيكٍ مُقْتَدِرٍ

Indeed, the Godwary will be amid gardens and streams. In a worthy abode, with an omnipotent King.[153]

153. Quran, 54:54–55.

If so, why do we have to go through all these material needs and attachments which become obstacles in our journey towards Almighty God?

The answer is that God gave us an intellect and the power to choose, and our movement must be within the correct choice. In order for us to attain perfection, we must overcome the obstacles and face the elements that oppose our happiness and perfection. We might fight against the problems and difficulties of life, and willingly choose the path towards perfection and happiness from the other paths and inclinations that are presented.

If we were to pursue this, we would reach the path of human perfection and the status of divine vicegerency. This is where Satanic elements and their presence can be seen and felt, because if someone did not enjoy the power of choice and was like an angel who has no ability other than obedience and submission to God, and also lacked the faculty of desire and anger, such a person would not be able to reach the status of divine vicegerency. This status of *al-khilāfah al-ilāhiyyah* is of course higher than the status of angels, and ultimately reaching this stage of human perfection.

While taking note of this reality that Almighty God created us to reach ultimate perfection and to become close to Him, at the same time in this world we are also inflicted with all these problems, difficulties and material attachments of which without them our material world cannot continue. So, what will save us from the mire of material attachments?

How can we remove these restrictions and shackles from ourselves so our souls can freely journey through the path of perfection and salvation, ridding ourselves of any material attachments? The answer is the best factor that can save us from the snare of these attachments is remembrance of God, and the best manifestation of remembrance of God is in the act of prayer. Therefore, when we say prayer is a factor for success, it means that prayer can remove someone from these contaminations and material attachments and save them from it all. They will be freed from Satan's captivation and carnal desires, and guided to the fundamental path of life, which is the path of human spiritual perfection.

In reality, a human being is an entity hovering in space, standing between two contradictory attractions, with each one wanting to draw this hovering entity towards itself.

The first attraction is the material attachments that always drag the human towards it, constantly drawing its attention and occupying it. If the human self is not disciplined and controlled, it will end up stuck in this mire from which it will be extremely difficult to extricate.

The second attraction is the divine spiritual attraction that occurs within the remembrance of God, prayer, veneration, and the presence of the heart. This attraction can save the human from the snare of material attachments and remove him from the mire of contaminations, darkness, and degeneration. The fundamental element for human success and what strengthens one's attention to God is prayer, accompanied with humility (*khushūʿ*) and veneration (*khuḍūʿ*) towards Him. This will keep one on the path, as the Almighty says:

﴿قَد أَفلَحَ المُؤمِنونَ ۝ الَّذينَ هُم في صَلاتِهِم خاشِعونَ﴾

Certainly, the faithful have attained salvation —those who are humble in their prayers.[154]

154. Quran, 23:1–2.

This is because prayer is the best element and format in manifesting remembrance of God, and it brings about perfection, steadfastness and consistency in remembrance. Prayer also prevents people from all vices and base acts, as the following verse says:

﴿إِنَّ الصَّلاَةَ تَنهىٰ عَنِ الفَحشاءِ وَالمُنكَرِ وَلَذِكرُ اللَّهِ أَكبَرُ﴾

Indeed, the prayer prevents indecencies and wrongs, and the remembrance of Allah is surely greater.[155]

In another verse the Almighty says, addressing Prophet Moses (ʿa):

﴿أَقِمِ الصَّلاَةَ لِذِكري﴾

Maintain the prayer for My remembrance.[156]

Prayer frees you from contaminations and veils of the self and from Satanic constraints. Prayer leads to the eradication of material and carnal attractions, and draws you to spiritual and divine attractions, turning towards the Sovereignty of God. This is why in Adhān and Iqāma prayer is introduced as an element for salvation.

Question Four: Considering that there are other deeds that could also lead to salvation, is it only prayer that leads to salvation?

Answer: When looking into the elements that lead to salvation, we perceive that prayer is a necessary condition to obtain salvation. Without prayer, no element and no other method can reach salvation. It is for this reason that when Quranic verses were revealed, describing those who have attained salvation (*al-mufliḥīn*), "prayer" was either

155. Quran, 29:45.
156. Quran, 20:14.

mentioned explicitly,[157] or more general expressions were used in the verse that also include prayer as well, like:

﴿وَاتَّقُوا اللَّهَ لَعَلَّكُم تُفلِحونَ﴾

And be wary of Allah so that you may be felicitous.[158]

Therefore, it is certainly the case that no person can attain the wariness of God without prayer.

As mentioned, prayer is a necessary condition (*sharṭ lāzim*) for salvation, but it is not a sufficient condition (*sharṭ kāfī*), in that prayer is not taken as a substitute for all the other duties and responsibilities placed on us. If someone was to pray day and night, but not uphold other obligations, like fasting, Hajj pilgrimage, jihad, enjoining the good and forbidding the wrong or seeking knowledge, they will not attain salvation, because the other obligations are also elements for salvation. What we must stress here is that from among all the elements that lead to salvation, prayer is not just a necessary condition, but also the most important and most effective of elements in obtaining it.

Question Five: In some narrations other deeds have been mentioned as the "best of deeds", like being martyred for the sake of God, like the following narration from the holy Prophet (ṣ):

فَوْقَ كُلِّ ذِي بِرٍّ بَرٌّ حَتَّى يُقْتَلَ اَلرَّجُلُ فِي سَبِيلِ اَللَّهِ فَإِذَا
قُتِلَ فِي سَبِيلِ اَللَّهِ فَلَيْسَ فَوْقَهُ بِرٌّ

---

157. As can be seen in the beginning of Sūrat-al-Baqarah, verse 5 and Sūrat-al-Mu'minūn, verse 1.

158. Quran, 3:200.

> For every virtue there is another higher virtue, until a man is slain for the sake of God, as there is no virtue higher than this.[159]

So, how can we say in Adhān and Iqāma "hasten to prayer" being the best deed, and why is prayer regarded as the best of deeds?

Answer: At first, the essential and significant aspects of prayer that make it surpass any other deed can be divided into three parts:

First: Prayer is the only obligatory duty that is obligatory for every person every day under all circumstances, and it is the only duty that can be performed in any state. Opposite to this, jihad is not always obligatory, and the possibility of partaking in jihad is not accessible for people all the time, either because there is no active war, or the necessary or sufficient circumstances are not available to partake in it.

It is feasible for someone to carry out all of their duties throughout their lifetime even if there is no war for them to fight. However, for prayer, it is obligatory for them to pray in the five allocated times in the day, along with praying recommended prayers as well. You can pray recommended prayers while working, traveling, on a boat, in a car, on a train or in a plane. If you are not able to pray the supererogatory prayers in their allocated time, you are able to perform them outside of their time, and you do not even need to be facing the qibla nor observe some of the other conditions that must be met for obligatory prayers.

As for fasting, it is only obligatory during the holy month of Ramadan, and if you are sick during this holy month, or have a valid excuse, you do not fast. You only redo the obligatory fasting days if the juristic exemption is no longer applicable to you, whereas with prayer

159. *Al-Kāfī*, v. 1, p. 348.

it is obligatory under all circumstances, even if you are sick and you cannot stand or sit, or even if you are drowning, you perform your prayer in whichever way you are able to.

Second: Another exceptional feature prayer has over all other acts of worship is that prayer must be done solely with the motive of worship and gaining nearness to Almighty God. The reality, spirit and essence of prayer is connecting with God, and this attention and submission to God crystallises in the invocations and actions in the prayer.

To further explain, worship means connecting with God, and an act is considered worship only if it is done with the intention of being for God and in worship of Him, including the connection with God. So, if someone was to do something very good, but without the intention of gaining closeness to God (*qaṣd al-qurbā*) or as an act of worship, then this particular act would not be considered as worship, nor result in any reward. It could have been done for the sake of craving fame, or any other motive, but not with the motive of worship and wanting to gain closeness to the Almighty.

However, if there is an act that is not apparently considered as worship, and it can be done with a non-worship motive, then it could have benefits, even if it is performed without intention of being for God or as worship. For example, someone can go to jihad with the intention of wanting to gain closeness to God and as an act of worship, and it is also possible to go to jihad with a non-Divine motive, in which their benefit will be in the spoils of war, or for protecting their country, or defending the onslaught of an enemy, or to bring back safety, or any other benefits.

The same is regarding fasting, even though it is an act of worship, if someone does it without intention of gaining closeness to God (*qaṣd al-qurbā*) and without the motive of worship, like it being for health reasons, then they will have the benefits, because they have performed something that does have benefits.

Another example is someone who gives to charity without intending to do so for the glory of God. While this charitable act is not worship, it is still positive in and of itself and will have many advantages, such as a clear conscience and protecting society from the dangers of theft, among other things. Such acts that can be done without intention of gaining closeness to God are considered as "accidental acts of worship" (*ʿibādāt ʿaraḍiyya*), because they can be done without a Godly motive, but still produce a reality and identity that has numerous benefits.

As for prayer, it is an act of worship in itself and cannot occur without intention of gaining nearness to God and without a Godly motive. In other words, it is not like fasting in which if done without "*qaṣd al-qurbā*" it will still have a benefit. If prayer is done without the intention of gaining nearness, it will be useless and futile, with no benefit at all. Every single act in prayer and every movement and statement are done as worship and showing servitude to Almighty God, as prayer is a manifestation of connecting with God. This is why prayer is the best of all acts of worship.

Third: Another distinctive quality prayer has over other acts of worship is that the person praying is able to have complete attention to this worship and remember God and not pay attention to anything else at all. Of course, this high level of presence of the heart and absolute attention to He who is being worshipped is not something achieved by normal people, but prayer itself does have this ability where someone is able to completely turn their attention to God. This is the state of prayer that God's saints and His elite are blessed with, as they focus on nothing but God. As for all other acts of worship, they do not have this capacity, and one cannot gain absolute attention in remembering God like prayer.

In these other acts of worship, in addition to the presence of the heart and turning to God, there are other things one must think of or do. For example, jihad against the enemy is an act of worship, but while fighting one is not able to completely concentrate on God and nothing else. In addition to the importance of intention being for God and doing it as an act of worship, one must also pay attention to the enemy and surrounding circumstances, trying to be alert and cautious as much as possible in repelling and facing the enemy.

It is for this reason one is compelled to direct a part of their faculties to things other than God. In this case, the inability to concentrate on one point and focusing on multiple things all at once is something necessary that cannot be avoided. However, this is not the case with prayer, because in prayer a wayfaring believer is able to completely concentrate and totally direct their attention towards this act of worship. This is another reason why prayer is superior to any other act of worship.

These distinctive qualities we have mentioned about prayer make it better than any other act of worship or deed. Without doubt, other acts of worship do have their own distinctive qualities specific to them that cannot be overlooked, and prayer cannot be done as a substitute for them. Therefore, one must not assume that praying and doing recommended prayers will relieve them of other obligatory acts, or that they will no longer need them, or that this strong emphasis on prayer will lead them to abandon other important deeds.

Unfortunately, this is what happened in the beginning of Islam with the Second Caliph when expanding the territory of Muslim land. He wanted to encourage people to go to war and fight. He thought that if prayer was regularly announced numerous times per day in Adhān and Iqāma as "the best of deeds" (*khayr al-ʿamal*), people would no longer prioritise the importance of fighting the disbelievers and turn to prayer, due to it being "the best of deeds" instead of fighting. This is why the Second Caliph ordered "hasten to the best of deeds" be removed from Adhān and Iqāma, unaware that prayer can never in any form be substituted by any other duty or act of worship. All other acts of worship stay as obligatory duties that must be done, but prayer can never substitute fasting or jihad against the enemies of God, and fasting and jihad can never be substitutes for prayer.

The Wisdom Behind Reciting Quran in Prayer

After *Takbīratul-Iḥrām*, the person praying must recite Sūrat-al-Fātiḥa and then any other complete Sūra from the Holy Quran. According to Shīʿa belief, in an obligatory prayer it is impermissible to recite a Sūra that has an obligatory prostration in it.[160]

Here, there are two questions put forward:

1. Why is it obligatory for Muslims to recite the Quran in prayer?
2. Why does reciting of the Quran in prayer start with reciting Sūrat-al-Fātiḥa?

Coincidently, some people had asked these two questions to Imām al-Riḍā (ʿa), and he answered the first question by saying:

أُمِرَ ٱلنَّاسُ بِٱلْقِرَاءَةِ فِي ٱلصَّلَاةِ، لِئَلَّا يَكُونَ ٱلْقُرْآنُ

160. There are four Sūras in the Holy Quran that have a verse in it in which if recited it is obligatory to prostrate. These Sūras are referred to as *suwar al-ʿazāʾim*, and they are: Sūrat-al-Sajda [32], verse 15, Sūrah Fuṣṣilat [41], verse 37, Sūrat-al-Najm [53], verse 62 and Sūrat-al-ʿAlaq [96], verse 19. (Tr.)

مَهْجُوراً مُضَيَّعاً، وَ لِيَكُونَ مَحْفُوظاً مَدْرُوساً، فَلاَ يَضْمَحِلَّ وَلاَ يُجْهَلَ

People were commanded to recite Quran in prayer so that the Quran is not neglected and abandoned, and so that it be remembered and taught for it not to be erased and forgotten.[161]

Therefore, it is necessary for Muslims to recite a part of the Quran every day. Almighty God made it obligatory for those who pray, to recite the Quran ten times each day in their prayer, because of how important it is to connect with the Quran and preserve its message. If this was not the case and if reciting the Quran was not obligatory in prayer, most Muslims would have cut their relationship with the Quran, which is the greatest gift and divine blessing upon mankind.

The only way to happiness in this life and the afterlife is through the Quran. Muslims must always maintain this unwavering connection to the Quran and in all circumstances. People will gradually become accustomed to and friendly with the Quran's language and recitation after such a connection is made with it. As a result, the foundation for comprehending Quranic ideas is laid, making it easier to follow the Quran's instructions.

However, if the Quran was not obligatory to recite in prayer, and reciting the Quran only remained recommended, most people will not have that motive to recite it. If such a path was closed, then the wisdom behind descending of the Quran, which is human guidance, would never be achieved in practice.

---

161. Al-Ṣadūq, *Man lā Yaḥḍurahū al-Faqīh* v. 1, p. 310.

As for the answer to the second question, which was why Almighty God made it obligatory for people praying to recite each day ten times Sūrat-al-Fātiḥa, the Imām al-Riḍā (ʿa) replied:

وَإِنَّمَا بَدَأَ بِالْحَمْدِ دُونَ سَائِرِ اَلسُّوَرِ، لِأَنَّهُ لَيْسَ شَيْءٌ مِنَ
اَلْقُرْآنِ وَاَلْكَلاَمِ جُمِعَ فِيهِ مِنْ جَوَامِعِ اَلْخَيْرِ وَاَلْحِكْمَةِ مَا
جُمِعَ فِي سُورَةِ اَلْحَمْدِ

And prayer commences with [Sūrat-al-Ḥamd and not any other Sūra because there is nowhere in the Quran or any statement where all the good and wisdom is combined like how it is combined in Sūrat-al-Ḥamd.[162]

In addition to this, we can understand that the important and necessary connection with the Quran comes from God's mercy and grace towards us so that through the Quran we can benefit from His infinite teachings and realities in our path towards happiness and attaining perfection. If we were to just suffice with supplication alone in prayer, we would be deprived from the blessings of the Quran.

However, because we are Muslim, we have pledged an oath to God that we will move in the path of acquiring His satisfaction and achieve His will. We chose His path to reach happiness. Almighty God also made the Quran the only way to connect with Him so that we may reach the status of His proximity, through benefiting and practicing this Heavenly Book.

---

162. Ibid.

Chapter Five

An Accepted Prayer

While explaining a Ḥadīth Qudsī, Imām al-Ṣādiq ('a) mentions some of the conditions and effects of an accepted prayer. He says:

يَا اِبْنَ جُنْدَبٍ قَالَ اَللَّهُ جَلَّ وَعَزَّ فِي بَعْضِ مَا أَوْحَى: إِنَّمَا أَقْبَلُ اَلصَّلاَةَ مِمَّنْ يَتَوَاضَعُ لِعَظَمَتِي وَيَكُفُّ نَفْسَهُ عَنِ اَلشَّهَوَاتِ مِنْ أَجْلِي وَيَقْطَعُ نَهَارَهُ بِذِكْرِي وَلاَ يَتَعَظَّمُ عَلَى خَلْقِي وَيُطْعِمُ اَلْجَائِعَ وَيَكْسُو اَلْعَارِيَ وَ يَرْحَمُ اَلْمُصَابَ وَيُؤْوِي اَلْغَرِيبَ; فَذَلِكَ يُشْرِقُ نُورُهُ مِثْلَ اَلشَّمْسِ. أَجْعَلُ لَهُ فِي اَلظُّلْمَةِ نُوراً، وَفِي اَلْجَهَالَةِ حِلْماً، أَكْلَؤُهُ بِعِزَّتِي وَأَسْتَحْفِظُهُ مَلاَئِكَتِي، يَدْعُونِي فَأُلَبِّيهِ، وَيَسْأَلُنِي فَأُعْطِيهِ، فَمَثَلُ ذَلِكَ اَلْعَبْدِ عِنْدِي كَمَثَلِ جَنَّاتِ اَلْفِرْدَوْسِ لاَ يُسْبَقُ أَثْمَارُهَا وَلاَ تَتَغَيَّرُ عَنْ حَالِهَا

O Ibn Jundab,[163] among that which God the Mighty the Venerable revealed was: I only accept the prayer of those

163. 'Abdullah ibn Jundab al-Bajalī al-Kūfī was among the companions and narrators of Imām al-Ṣādiq ('a), Imām al-Kāẓim ('a) and Imām al-

> who are humble before My Glory, and who keep themselves away from desires for My sake, and who spend their day remembering Me, and who do not become haughty over My creation. Those who feed the hungry, dress the undressed, have mercy upon those afflicted and give refuge to strangers. Their light will shine just like the light of the sun. I will grant them light in darkness and patience in ignorance. I will guard him with My honour, and have My angels protect him. He will supplicate to Me and I will fulfil for him, and he will ask Me and I will grant him. This kind of servant for Me is like the Paradise of *Firdaws*, its merits will never decrease, and its condition will never change.[164]

Conditions of an Accepted Prayer

Taking into consideration this above ḥadīth, we can explain the conditions and effects of an accepted prayer in the following points:

1. Humility in Front of the Exaltedness of the Almighty Lord

One who prays must remember the exaltedness of Almighty God. The more you are blessed with knowing God's magnificence, the humbler you will be in His presence, further perceiving more and more how insignificant and weak you are.

2. Avoiding Lusts to Please God

The second condition for the person praying is to stay away from all forms of impious desires and lusts for the sake of God. You say: "O God, I am avoiding this for Your sake, and I keep myself away from

---

Riḍā (ʿa). He is regarded as reliable and trustworthy in his narrations. (Tr.)

164. *Biḥār al-Anwār*, v. 78, p. 285, ḥ. 1. *Mizān al-Ḥikma*, v. 4, p. 3388.

desires and sin." It is very similar to when at times you avoid things that you like for the sake of your friends, you can also do that for the sake of God and stay away from unlawful desires and avoid them.

There is of course an inverse relationship between performing prayer in the correct form and pursuing unlawful desires, in that the better one performs their prayer the further they will be from unlawful desires. The opposite is also the case, where the more one pursues lusts, the further they will be from prayer.[165]

How beautiful did the Quran explain this, when discussing some previous nations and after mentioning a few of the Prophets, saying:

﴿إِذَا تُتلَىٰ عَلَيهِم آيَاتُ الرَّحمٰنِ خَرّوا سُجَّدًا وَبُكِيًّا﴾

When the signs of the All-beneficent were recited to them, they would fall down weeping in prostration.[166]

Almighty God then says:

﴿فَخَلَفَ مِن بَعدِهِم خَلفٌ أَضاعُوا الصَّلاةَ وَاتَّبَعُوا الشَّهَواتِ فَسَوفَ يَلقَونَ غَيًّا﴾

But they were succeeded by an evil posterity who neglected the prayer and followed [their base] appetites. So they will soon encounter [the reward of] perversity.[167]

If someone wants to know why they are not feeling that connection with God or do not have any amiability with God in prayer as it should

165. In other words, there is an ongoing battle between prayer and debauchery and wrongdoings, and whenever there is truce in one side, this will lead to fire in the other side.

166. Quran, 19:58.

167. Quran, 19:59.

be, then they must look into how much they are attached to unlawful desires and invalid thoughts.

3. Constant Remembrance of God

The third condition is for the person who prays to start their day with remembrance of God. There are people who constantly remember God, in every instance, never forgetting Him at all:

﴿رِجالٌ لا تُلهيهِم تِجارَةٌ وَلا بَيعٌ عَن ذِكرِ اللَّهِ﴾

Men whom neither trading nor sale (business) can divert from the remembrance of Allah.[168]

Almighty God has people who will never allow any worldly act to come between them and remembering Him. When discussing the human ability to remember God while being occupied with worldly affairs, the late ʿAllāmah Ṭabāṭabāʾī said:

> The same way as loss of a loved one or being in love with someone would not prevent us from performing our regular daily activities, as we could do our work but still be remembering them, in this same way people of God also constantly remember God in all circumstances.

4. Humility Towards God's Servants

The same way as one must be humble and subordinate to God, they must also be far away from showing haughtiness towards God's servants.[169] Based on this, another condition of prayer being accepted is avoiding arrogance over God's creation.

---

168. Quran, 24:37.

169. Humility towards God's servants naturally stems from humility in front of God because God's servants are a manifestation of His power

5. Feeding the Hungry

Another condition is that if you see someone hungry and unable to obtain food, then you feed them, and this is one form of zakāt. In Quranic terminology, zakāt is not restricted to the obligatory zakāt that is related to specific wealth. The concept of zakāt in the Quran is spending for the sake of God. In Islam, there is obligatory zakāt and there is recommended zakāt. Obligatory zakāt is related to certain wealth, but recommended zakāt includes almsgiving, charity, and similar acts. We never see prayer and zakāt separated from each other. In the Quran, Almighty God says about Prophet Jesus ('a):

﴿وَأَوصاني بِالصَّلاةِ وَالزَّكاةِ ما دُمتُ حَيًّا﴾

And He has enjoined me to [maintain] the prayer and to [pay] the zakāt as long as I live.[170]

Therefore, spending as charity (*infāq*) on the poor is another condition for acceptance of prayer.

6. Clothing the Unclothed

Another condition for prayer being accepted is if you see someone without clothes who cannot clothe themselves you clothe them. Of course, this does not mean that the person is completely naked and has nothing at all to cover himself for this to be applicable to them. What is meant here is that if someone needs clothes, we provide for them.

---

and wisdom. Therefore, being outwardly humble to creation is in reality being humble to the Creator..

170. Quran, 19:31.

7. Solidarity with those Afflicted with a Calamity

Another condition for acceptance of prayer is to show solidarity and care to those who have been afflicted with a calamity.

8. Sheltering Strangers

A condition for prayer being accepted is if we come across someone who has no shelter or home, we must try as much as we can to facilitate accommodation for them.

Effects of an Accepted Prayer

1. An Illuminated Face

Those who observe the conditions of an accepted prayer, their face will illuminate in the spiritual realm just like the sun illuminates over this world. Those who have an inner eye will be able to see this radiance in this world as well. Most people might not see this radiance, but there are those who have touched into their inner eye and whenever they see someone's face, they know if this person is among the sinners or among the worshippers. Therefore, among the creational (*Takwīnī*) effects of worship is the illumination of the heart and spirit.

2. Removing Darkness in Life

Almighty God lightens up the darkness of the life of every worshipper whose prayer He accepts. This has been mentioned in the Holy Quran, where the Almighty says:

﴿يَا أَيُّهَا الَّذِينَ آمَنُوا اتَّقُوا اللَّهَ وَآمِنُوا بِرَسُولِهِ يُؤْتِكُم كِفْلَيْنِ مِن رَحْمَتِهِ وَيَجْعَل لَّكُمْ نُورًا تَمْشُونَ بِهِ وَيَغْفِرْ لَكُمْ وَاللَّهُ غَفُورٌ رَحِيمٌ﴾

O you who have faith! Be wary of Allah and have faith in His Apostle. He will grant you a double share of His mercy and give you a light to walk by, and forgive you, and Allah is all-forgiving, all-merciful.[171]

For those who fear God and are wary of Him, when they are distressed from the darkness of this world, He will grant them light, even physical light. There have been individuals who have lost sight, but they were able to recite the Quran. There is one case I heard from very trustworthy people about a janitor in Madrasah Marwī in Tehran[172] who had once witnessed two shining lights in one of the school's rooms. When he went to the room, he saw a blind man reciting the Quran and the two lights were shining from his eyes over the Quran.

3. Forbearance Towards the Ignorant

If humans live in this world, whether they like it or not they will face individuals who will treat them with ignorance and exhaust all their patience and tolerance. In these kinds of trying circumstances, one must control himself and if Almighty God accepts the prayer of a worshipper, He will grant this person forbearance and patience to use to control himself in front of mistreatment of people.

4. Protection by God's Angels

Almighty God will protect His worshippers with His angels if staying alive is to their advantage.

5. Answering Requests

Almighty God will answer their prayers and fulfil their requests.

---

171. Quran, 57:28.

172. Madrasah Marwī is a famous Seminary school in Tehran established in 1231/1816 AH/CE.

6. Joy and Happiness

Such a worshipper is like the flowers and fruits of Heaven that never wilt or diminish, always live and fresh. The rational interpretation for this is that a worshipper who becomes one with religious teachings and never affected by change will absorb the religious teachings and it will become a fixed state within them and their spirit.

A Final Question

Here we pose the following question. In this narration:

اَلصَّلاَةِ مِعْرَاجُ اَلْمُؤْمِنِ.

Prayer is the ascension of the believer.[173]

And based on what the Almighty has said in the following verse:

﴿إِنَّ الصَّلاةَ تَنهىٰ عَنِ الفَحشاءِ وَالمُنكَرِ﴾

Indeed, the prayer prevents indecencies and wrongs.[174]

Why is it that although we pray, we still do not see its effects in our existence? Why don't we even once feel our prayer becoming our ascension and us ascending with our prayer? Why is it that we still commit vile acts? Why don't we experience the tens of effects of prayer that have been mentioned in verses and narrations?

The answer is that we, in reality, are not praying. Instead, what we are doing is just performing the outer form that resembles prayer. When we finish our prayer, and realise we just prayed, did we really pray?

---

173. *Biḥār al-Anwār*, vol. 79, p. 303, ḥ. 2.

174. Quran, 29:45.

There are many issues we do not think about in other times, but we wait for prayer time to display them and think about them, occupying our minds about them during prayer. For example, if we wanted to teach a lesson after the Maghribayn prayer, and because we didn't have enough time to prepare for the lesson, we would use the Maghribayn prayer time to revise the lesson in our mind. Many people who engage in business, while they are praying, they think about their debts, their cheques, and their transactions. Are we able to refer to these kinds of examples as a true act of prayer?

Not only does our prayer not result in perfection, but we also need to repent because of them. In addition to our insolence and our sins, we must repent and seek God's forgiveness for this kind of worship and prayer. If a person were to get up and praise someone in front of other people, using words he himself does not understand, would that be considered as the praising of that individual, or insulting and mockery of them?

If someone wanted to show their love to you, using words and expressions like "I love you" or "I care for you", but you know what is in their heart and you know that they are just saying these words verbally, but their heart is somewhere else, they are not paying attention to any of the meanings in these words. How would you deal with them?

If someone was talking to you, but they are facing somewhere else, looking right, left and all around, would you not consider this to be a great insult and lack of respect? We must really ask: is our worship and our prayer an insult or worship?

There is a narration attributed to the holy Prophet (ṣ), saying:

أَمَا يَخَافُ ٱلَّذِي يُحَوِّلُ وَجْهَهُ فِي ٱلصَّلَاةِ أَنْ يُحَوِّلَ ٱللَّهُ وَجْهَهُ حِمَارًا

> Does he who moves his face around in prayer [distracted] not fear that God transforms his face into that of a donkey?[175]

When someone in prayer says "*Allāhu-Akbar*", testifying that God is greater than anything, but their mind is attached to someone or something else, this means that person or that thing for them is greater and more important than God. As a result, would this sentence being said, God forbid, be nothing other than mocking the Almighty? If someone were to praise and extol us, and we are certain that they do not believe in any word they say, would we not take what they say to be nothing but mockery?

He who with his tongue says "*Allāhu-Akbar*", but at the same time God sees his heart and knows that this is not what he really believes. Does this person not deserve to have his face transformed into that of a donkey?

When we are speaking with a normal person, we would not turn our face away from them, so has the Almighty, God forbid, become of less value than a normal person that when we speak to Him in our prayer, we turn our hearts away from Him and think of other things? Indeed, we must implore God and ask Him to forgive us for all the years we have prayed in these deficient ways. Yes, stated correctly, that He forgives our prayer, not our sins. Our prayer which was not true worship or correct prayer, but worship mixed with insult and mockery.

The Almighty says in the Holy Quran:

﴿يَا أَيُّهَا الَّذِينَ آمَنُوا لَا تَقْرَبُوا الصَّلَاةَ وَأَنتُمْ سُكَارَىٰ حَتَّىٰ
تَعْلَمُوا مَا تَقُولُونَ﴾

175. *Biḥār al-Anwār*, v. 81, p. 211, ḥ. 3.

> *O you who have faith! Do not approach prayer when you are intoxicated, [not] until you know what you are saying.* [176]

What is the value of the words of a drunkard? The intellect of an intoxicated person does not correctly function or perceive, nor do they completely comprehend what they are saying, even though they are uttering things. In this situation, if they are praising or extolling someone, what they say would have no value and nobody would pay any attention to it. "This is why Almighty God says: do not go to pray and do not converse with God while you are intoxicated, because what you say will have no value or credibility."

Even though this verse is related to intoxication and the inattentiveness that occurs from consuming alcohol, but by looking at the cause mentioned consequently in the verse "*until you know what you are saying*", this could address anyone who wants to pray while being inattentive and wanting to converse with God. A drunk person who does not comprehend what they are saying should not approach prayer, and anyone who is inattentive to God during prayer with their focus and mind somewhere else for that matter as they do not perceive what they are saying.

Therefore, the primary reason behind not correctly benefiting from our prayer and not feeling perfection through our prayer is because we are not praying the real prayer. Our hope is to anticipate having done what our duty is, and the least is that when we are in our graves or on Judgment Day, we will not be asked or judged, why did we not pray?

However, there is no doubt that we have not gained from our prayer any perfection or spiritual benefit. When we become very holy, wanting to be pious and righteous, we focus on improving our recitation and *tajwīd*, praying with a pleasant voice. We think that the

---

176. Quran, 4:43.

most that we should be attentive to in our prayer is to pronounce the letters in the correct form, unaware that this is only the outer aspect of the prayer and its form.

As for the reality and spirit of prayer, that is something else. What is seen in the outer form of prayer is only an outer shell, but that which elevates a person is when their heart and spirit are connected with the essence of Almighty God. The reality and spirit of prayer is the attention of the heart, without which the prayer will be a dead body with no soul. Would there be any hope in this dead form having any result or movement? This prayer that is such a priceless gem that cannot be replaced is in front of us and accessible to us but unfortunately, we pass through the act carelessly not giving it enough value or active regard and thought.

For many people, when they pursue the path of perfection and spiritual wayfaring, they passionately look for that mentor who will tell them the hidden secret or tell them not to inform others of the secret, or give them a *dhikr*, or teach it to them. If there was something in this path more important than prayer, would it be possible for God to keep it from us or be parsimonious in giving it to His worshippers?

Almighty God, who sent the Quran as a mercy unto mankind and sent the most honourable of His creation as a guide, would He conceal the secret for our guidance, our perfection and our happiness? Then someone else other than a Prophet or Ahlul Bayt (ʿa) would come and give it to a select few through special symbols in a hidden place?

If there was something more important and more effective than prayer in this path of human perfection, God would certainly have emphasised on it in the Quran. If there was a deed more important than prayer, Prophets and divine saints would have given it more importance than anything else. Why did the Commander of the

Faithful Imām ʿAlī (ʿa) choose prayer from among all the deeds and all forms of worship, as he would perform one thousand units of prayer in a day and night? This prayer that in its outer form is nothing other than repeating of words and movements.

During the life of Imām ʿAlī (ʿa), he would do this repetition each day a thousand times, and we ask about this meaning or message that he wanted to convey to us in this regard. Why was Imām ʿAlī (ʿa) so fixated in not abandoning these one thousand units, and he would also pray the supererogatory prayers as well, and also recite the Quran, while moving, or while ploughing, farming or digging wells.[177] In brief, we have not yet comprehended the value and importance of prayer, because there is nothing more important and better than prayer from among all the deeds that bring us closer to God. The problem with our prayer is that it is not a real prayer. If it was a real prayer, we would see its effects and blessings, either in this worldly life, or on the level of spiritual excellence and perfection.

---

177. We know that the recommended prayers do not have most of the conditions of an obligatory prayer. For example, it is not required to face the qibla, or be still, or bow or prostrate on the ground, and other conditions. One is therefore able to pray the nāfila prayers in any state, and it could be that many of the prayers that Imām ʿAlī (ʿa) performed that reached one thousand were of this type. I myself have seen many scholars and great people pray this kind of prayer. In the past this was something very common because people did not have the transport facilities that we have with us today. It would take people a very long time when travelling from one place to another, and many scholars and great people would use this opportunity and pray nāfila prayers. May God have mercy upon my teacher, the late ʿAllāmah Ṭabāṭabāʾī, whom we would sometimes accompany from his place to where he taught. We would notice that he would pray nāfila prayers during the way. Or the late Sheikh Ghulāmreḍā Faqīh al-Khurāsānī (d. 1378 AH) who was one of our teachers in Yazd. Most of the time, he would pray nāfila prayers whenever he went from his home to the mosque, or from one place to another.

Our last word is to say:
Thanks be to Allah, Lord of Creation,
and may Allah bless our master Muhammad (ṣ)
and his Holy Progeny (ʿa).

www.ingramcontent.com/pod-product-compliance
Lightning Source LLC
Chambersburg PA
CBHW052141070526
44585CB00017B/1924
* 9 7 8 1 7 3 8 4 9 4 9 3 4 *